MEDIA AND MARGINALISATION: THE PERIPHERY VOICES

EDITED BY PROF. V. RATNAMALA & DR. SAYAN DEY

Contents

Contents

Foreword

Media and Marginalisation: The Periphery Voices

The representation of oppressed communities in media content and workspace is an important subject of research in media and communication studies. Many groups in Indian society are seen as inferior or marginal, and they are labelled as marginalised. The study of the portrayal of women, Dalits, Tribes, religious and linguistic minorities in India falls within the broad academic domain of Media and Margins. In India studying the representation of Women, Dalits, Scheduled Tribes, Religious and linguistic minorities comes under the broad research area of Media and Margins. According to Stuart Hall, "Representation is the production meaning in the minds of the people". Aside from the presence and absence of news about marginalized people in mainstream media, it is critical to examine how the media constructs meaning about marginalised communities and regions through its discourse.

The media is affecting our aesthetic, cultural, civic, social, political and economic outlook. Since media is an intricate part of the social matrix, it commands continual deliberation, discourse and debate in a myriad of timelines and settings. The media is seen as a crucial instrument for connecting the entire world. Media industry plays a crucial role in our country which happens to be the world's largest democracy. Any democratic society requires a free, objective, and professional media. Article 15 in the Constitution of India prohibits any discrimination on grounds of religion, race, caste, sex or place of birth. So it is the duty of the media to safeguard the fundamental rights of all its citizens by ensuring equal access and participation of all. Considering upper caste Hindu men dominate the mainstream media, the issue of representation automatically emerges. As a result, it is critical to examine the current state of media and representation. This edited collection's purpose is to bring together media experts from throughout the country to explore themes of marginality in media portrayals. This edited collection of articles will dive deeply into the dimensions of marginalisation, providing a scholarly platform for engaging and re-engaging with the realities of marginalisation, the periphery voices. These contributions highlight the need of using diverse methodologies and disciplinary lenses to a complicated and serious social issue. The collection is distinctive in that it includes both theoretical viewpoints and case studies on media representation of Northeast India, women and media and gender in media.

Preface

List of the Contributors

    1. Dr. Anjani Kumar Jha, Associate Professor and Head, Department of Media
Studies, Mahatma Gandhi Central University, Motihari, Bihar
2. Dr. Deepika, Faculty, Department of Media Studies, Gurugram University
3. Dr. Dheeraj Kumar, Assistant Professor, Dept. of Mass Communication, Mizoram
University
4. Dr. Shweta Chaudhary, Faculty, Department of Media Studies, Gurugram
University
5. Dr.K.S.Ragini, Assistant Professor, School of Media Studies, Malayalam
University,
Kerala
6. Dr.Sayan Dey, Assistant Professor, Dept. of Mass Communication, Mizoram
University
7. Mr. Anuj, PhD Research Scholar, Dept. of Mass Communication, Mizoram
University
8. Mr. Souvik Acharya, PhD Research Scholar in Mass Communication, Dept. of
Media Studies, Mahatma Gandhi Central University, Motihari Bihar
9. Mr.David Lalhmachhuana , Research Scholar, Dept. of Mass
Communication,
Mizoram University
10. Ms. Prachi Malhotra, Ph.D scholar, Amity school of communication, Amity
university-Noida
11. Ms. Aakriti Kohli, PhD Scholar, Centre for Media Studies, School of
Social Sciences,
Jawaharlal Nehru University, New Delhi
12. Ms. Champa Devi, Research Scholar, Department of Mass
Communication, Rajiv Gandhi
University, Arunachal Pradesh, India
13. Ms. Chitralekha Agrawal , PhD Research Scholar, Dept. of Mass
Communication,

Mizoram University

14. Ms. Epciba Immanuvel, former student, Dept. of Electronic Media, Pondicherry
University

15. Ms. Ereda Lourembam, Research Scholar, Department of Mass Communication,
Manipur University, Canchipur.

16. Ms. Priyanga, Post graduate student, Department of Journalism and Communication, University of Madras

17. Ms. Riya Maurya, PhD Research Scholar, Dept. of Mass Communication, Mizoram
University

Contents

Media Representation of Northeast India

1. 'Zorami: The Redemption Song' As A Resistance Text
Ms. Meghana V Goshi

2. Coverage of North Eastern News in Indian media: A Study on the Trends of
Representation
Shanatombi Wangkheimayum and Ganesh Sethi

3. Media Representation of North-East India: A Print Media analysis
Souvik Acharya and Dr. Anjani Kumar Jha

4. Representation Of Meitei Pangals (Muslim Minorities) In Television Coverage And Newsroom In Manipur
Ereda Lourembam

Women and Media

5. OTT Platforms and the Sensorium on the Smartphone Screen: Notes from
Women's Perspectives
Aakriti Kohli

6. Emerging Corporate Communication Strategies and Communication Initiatives among Corporate firms for ensuring Women friendly workspace during Covid Pandemic: A Case study based on an IT firm.
Dr.K.S.Ragini

7. A Study of Men Perception on Dauntless Depiction of Women in Indian Web Series
Riya Maurya and Dheeraj Kumar

Acknowledgements

'ZORAMI: THE REDEMPTION SONG' AS A RESISTANCE TEXT Meghana V Goshi

Introduction to Text

For any community, recognition becomes very significant. Whereas in a democratic rule this recognition and spacing for one's identity is pushed to the periferi. As we observe in India itself, the northeast is a melting pot of diversities yet the government is unable to accept and provide complete support to them. To ponder on this note the present research article focuses on the text, *Zorami: The Redemption Song*, penned by Malsawmi Jacob. The text denies the continuous reception of no validation from the central forces; and also brings forth the step motherly treatment inherited at the mercy of the then Assam province. The fragmented narrative structure through the lens of the female protagonist, Zorampari makes the screams and shrieks back to life for the readers. Zorampari, shortly referred to as Zorami is not just going through the process of redemption but also is seen to describe all those scars felt by the common Mizos during the bloody two decades of insurgency. Zorami herself tormented by molestation speaks of the frightening and coerced conditions that the fellow Mizo women have endured. Series of violations to this ethnicity are covered by the author explicitly in the text. The droppings of hundreds of bombs on Aizawl and its outskirts by the centre is another poignant wound for the Mizos being recorded in the narrative. The novel parallely creates a history to the Mizo community specifically in formation of its state. The much feared Famine or Mautam and the inevitable MNF proceedings are also documented in this novel. Amidst of all these Zorami posits the patriarchal dominance in Mizo society along with the mutual support gained by the new religion on the soil of Mizoram, Christinity. Surrounding these topics from the text, the reader gets to distinguish the disappearance of Mizo identity through the various cultural, political and geographical exploitation on the common Mizo folks. This attempt to erase the Mizo identity makes the community become resistant to their oppressors. One such attempt is made by writing *Zorami: The Redemption Song* by Malsawmi Jacob.

Major elements of the Text

The constant threat to one identity gives rise to a more dangerous resistance and the same was followed by the Mizo people after the independence of India. The resistance of Mizos are broadly divided into four categories. The first resistance started with the opposition to the dominance of Assamese culture on the Mizo speaking ones. The language of Assamese is completely an alien language to the Mizos. Neither could they understand the script or could they communicate the same orally. Before the formation of Mizoram on February 20th 1987 they were under the jurisdiction of the then Assam province. Hence Assamese became a burden to the Mizos when it was declared as the official language in the entire region. The lines in the chapter 4, *A Plague of Rat*, "Assamese *tawng*", "Because the state rulers are trying to force us to use it for all important matters. But we don't know the language and most of us will not be able to learn it even if we try. That means we Mizo people would become like fools in our own homeland." (35) clearly states the fear of Mizos how they will be denied and kept out of all the vital affairs of the land and how there would be a threat of not having even a Mizo representative for their problems either.

This problem only was noticed when the second issue of the ecology surfaced. Mizoram is widely known for the growth of bamboo shoots along with Manipur and Tripura and also has become a victim by nature once in every fifty years.The blossoming of the bamboo shoots once in five decades increases population of the rodents in a rapid manner and finally these rodents attack on the yield. Since Mizoram has rice as its staple food, in the agrarian sector rice is the major grown crop. Hence each and every morsel of rice is finished by the rats and the Mizo people have to live at the mercy of the Assam government. The very first negligence paved the way for Mizos to understand their position and they went in resistance against the Assamese language and culture also equally; and these resistant feeling is very clear in the same chapter 4, when Zorami's mother exasperates "The famine is only beginning and you are already starving." (33)This concept of losing the Mizo culture and ethnicity by the Mizos made them realise and finally act in a resistant manner, eventually forming Mizo National Front (MNF) in 1950s by PuLaldenga from the former Mizo National Famine Front (MNFF). Both the violent situation of Mautam and the dominance of Assam culture led to a series of insurgency against the central forces. As a result the innocent Mizos had to bear the brunt of getting bombed in their own homelnd. The bombing was not just once but a repetiotion to destroy the strength of thMizo rebels and hence was numerously dropped. In chapter 12, *Alarm Bells,*Zari's Father's saying makes it coherent, "They're likely to return. Get ready, we have to flee. Let's go to the forest", "Take the food along, we'll eat when we reach a safer place" (89) evokes terror in the minds of the readers. These bombs were of combustible types and hence everything of the Mizos in their house was transformed to ashes; thus making their condition more pitiable refugees in their own land. Henceforth besides insurgencies even the counter insurgencies have created havoc among the Mizo community. The novel remarks about the misbehaviour and maltreatment meant for the Mizos alone by the army chiefs.

The resistance in the work is not just for the external forces but also to the inner society of the Mizo system. The chapter 7 *Where Angels Fear to Tread*, states the incident of Zorami finding her suitable suitor, Sanga who later becomes her husband. Amidst all these matchmaking we see a firm and rigid patriarchal coercion on the women folk even in Mizo society. The command of Zorami's father to agree for the suitor is resisted by Zorami with a resistance call, "You didn't have to say that! As if I didn't know I'm damaged! As if I didn't know I'm good for nothing!" (55). This is a staunch and direct resistance of women against the male pressures unlike the other helpless resistance and rejections.The narrative points out resistance to both the viscous patriarchal norms and also to the shady characters in the army and also the Mizo Front. The character Ralkapa is one such character who transforms from the position of a victim to a victimizer in order to save his own life. The chapter 8 *What Man has Made of Man* and chapter 14, *Downward Slide* chalks out this Survival of fittest policy of Ralkapa. Between the direct calls of resistance and screams we do come across such references as to say no and resist to such presence of soldiers either. Similar shady characters are even present among the army too. In the chapter 18, *Survival and Nightmares* Malsawmi Jacob lists the heinous offences committed by Majors and officers from the army against the villagers, and rebellion family members. There is a tear jerking instance where a rebellion's wife and sister are taken captive, leaving behind the two month old baby boy alone at home the entire night. A destined death of the infant and the women eventually losing their sanity is the impact of the barbarous officers. Further in the same chapter the lines, "Our village had a harrowing time last night. He had forced another young girl. She cried aloud all night, and none of us who heard her cries could sleep. It is high time this misualpa, the wicked man, is punished." (118) clearly triggers trepidation and uneasiness even to read. These are some significant resistance present in the text, *Zorami*.

Secondary Texts

Zorami is not the only text to bring in such resistance. We also have other narratives from the northeast particularly. Zorami in several parts of the texts consciously speak of the peace and intellectual resistance which would provide them *"Zelenna! Freedom!"*(61) Chapter 8 again, guides the Mizo folks and directs the readers as to how violence has no space of hope anymore by the quotes, "If we start violence, our people will suffer terribly. Mind you, we will not be treated like the youngest child. We will be punished like stepsons. Just mark my words. Do you think the Indian government will hold their peace if we capture its offices? They will send battalions of army men to subdue us. Blood will flow in our land." (64) In resemblance to such narratives we also have other writers contributing through peaceful negotiations and intellectual activism. Several types of resistance are available and the same is exercised by various other writers too. The stalwart, Kaka D. Iralu, a prominent Naga activist and writer has contributed a lot to Naga Nationalism. The work *The Naga Saga: A Historical Account of the Fifty-Two year Indo Naga War and the Story of Those who were never allowed to tell it* was never accepted to be published by anybody hence he is seen to manage the publication of truth by himself. This is also a kind of resistance text in the backdrop of insurgency.

TesmulaAo too falls parallel to such resistance writings in her works; specially as an ethnographer she aims for a redemption of the naga community too. *These Hills Called Homes: stories from a War Zone* adds to the resistance spirit of the north east insurgency movement. With several other works by the remaining states under insurgency from the northwingemphasises the power of intellectual resistance with writers like Eastern Kire (*Mari*) from Nagaland,IndiraGoswami in regional language and

AruniKashyap's texts from Assam on the context of insurgency; even the writings of Mamang Dai from Arunachal pradesh underscores the the art of writing as resistance and gaining a larger audience across the globe.

Conclusion

Finally we see *Zorami*as not just a resistance which questions the authoritative tone from the mainstream but also a rebellious text which focuses on the minute internal discrimination faced by the common Mizos specially in terms of gender inequality and in search of peace. The author outrightly voices against the atrocities encountered by the Mizo society, both Mizos and Non-Mizos. Thus, the text posits as a resistance text and calls for the much-required peace.

Work Cited

Ao, Temsula. *These Hills Called Home: Stories from a War Zone*. Zubaan, 2006.

"Backflap." Tribune India, 6 February 2022, <https://www.tribuneindia.com/news/book-reviews/backflap-367410.2022>.Web.

"Big Bridge Press - BIOS - F to L." Big Bridge, <http://bigbridge.org/BB18/bios/bios-F-to-L.html>.Web.

Dai, Mamang. ESCAPING THE LAND.Speaking Tree, 2021. Kindle stores. Web.

Goshi, Meghana. *"Quest for Mizo Identity" in Malsawmi Jacob's Novel Zorami: The Redemption Song*. Smashwords, All India Forum for English Students Scholars and Trainers, 2022.

Hanghal, Ninglun. "Meet Malsawmi Jacob - First Mizo Author to Write an English LanguageNovel." The Better India, 12 June 2016, <https://www.thebetterindia.com/57733/giving-words-voice-mizo-women/>.Web.

"History of Christianity in Mizoram." Wikipedia, <https://en.wikipedia.org/wiki/History_of_Christianity_in_Mizoram>.Web.

Jacob, Malsawmi. Zorami: A Redemption Song. Edited by Varghese V. Ampat, PrimaloguePublishing Media Private Limited, 2015. Print.

Kashyap, Aruni. How to Tell the Story of an Insurgency: Fifteen Tales from Assam.

HarperCollins India, 2020. Print.

Kire, Easterince. *Mari*. HarperCollins Publishers India, 2010.

LalthanglianaB., and KalapanaPalkhiwala. Culture and folklore of Mizoram.PublicationsDivision Ministry of Information & Broadcasting, 2005.Google Books.

"Mautam."Wikipedia, <https://en.wikipedia.org/wiki/Mautam>.Web.

"Mizoram: About Mizoram." Veethi, <https://www.veethi.com/places/mizoram-state-18.htm>.Web.

"Mizoram Peace Accord." Wikipedia, <https://en.wikipedia.org/wiki/Mizoram_Peace_Accord>.Web.

"Mizoram."Wikipedia, <https://en.wikipedia.org/wiki/Mizoram#Etymology>.Web.

Pachua, L K. "Being Mizo: identity and belonging in Northeast India." *Asian Ethnicity*, 2014.

Patton, Jasmine. "Contemporary Naga Writings' Reclamation Of Culture And History Through Orality." *The Curious Reader*, 26 July 2019, https://www.thecuriousreader.in/features/naga-writings/. Accessed 15 April 2022.

Students, Naga."Remembering Kaka D. Iralu - Shillong." RAIOT, Tata Institute of Social Sciences, Mumbai., 11 April 2020, <https://raiot.in/remembering-kaka-d-iralu/>.Web.

CHAPTER TWO

COVERAGE OF NORTH EASTERN NEWS IN INDIAN MEDIA: A STUDY ON THE TRENDS OF REPRESENTATION

Shanatombi Wangkheimayum & Ganesh Sethi

COVERAGE OF NORTH EASTERN NEWS IN INDIAN MEDIA: A STUDY ON THE TRENDS OF REPRESENTATION

Shanatombi Wangkheimayum & Ganesh Sethi

1. INTRODUCTION

"To effectively communicate, we must realize that we are all different in the way we perceive the world and use this understanding as a guide to our communication with others"- Anthony Robbins

The urge to communicate is like uncontrollable genetic trade that humans inherited from their parents and ancestors, communication may seem like a simple process that can be completed within a framework that involved the sender, channels, and receiver. In contradiction, the process of communication is must complex, if the right message is not reached out the consequences are no lesser than "peeling the onion". For example, an infant's cry is a way to communicate to signal that he/she is hungry, uncomfortable, or neither of the above two options but his/her way to seek attention. Man connects through communication hence; it is one of the tools to hold the relations between human beings whether it is in terms of developing a personal relationship or maintaining a professional relationship.

With the evolution and increasing population of different cultures and communities, there is a rapid need for cross-cultural communication to inculcate a sense of harmonious cohabitation in society. To achieve that level of understanding among the people from various segments of the world, media inclusion and intervention become very essential in our lives. Mass media is the only medium that helps in communicating and connecting the sea of audiences around the globe.

The origin of 'Mass media' can be traced back to the times when 'dramas' were performed in ancient cultures to entertain and inform a large audience. At present, mass media have branched out to different forms which include Print media (books, magazines, newspapers); Broadcasting media (movies, radio, television, recordings), and Internet (blogs, podcasts, websites, etc.).

Enter Caption

The contribution made by progressionist like Johannes Gutenberg and Andrew Weinreich brings out many new faces in the media ecosystem. Despite rapid growth in both Broadcasting and New Media, the Print media has not lost its luster. Till today many readers consider Newspapers to be the most reliable source of information. Thus, it can be concluded that different form of media may be poles apart in characters but serves the same goal that is "infotainment".

1.1 Media Scenario in India

Media the 'fourth pillar of democracy also served as hawk-eyed for the people. Indian media consumers have access to multiple forms of media like Print media, Electronic Media, and New Media. Media consumers' exposure to amalgamated media forms, India is home to the second-largest print market in the world.

India's print media history can be traced back to the time of publication of the Bengal Gazette in 1780 by James Augustus Hickey from Calcutta and considered the father of the Indian Press. In the late 18th and 19th centuries, Indian newspapers were in their golden era when the people experienced the courageous work of James Silk Buckingham, the editor of 'The Calcutta Chronicle'. The social reformer Raja Ram Mohan Roy's contribution to Indian language journalism was unparalleled. The history of the Indian freedom struggle will be incomplete without the intervention of the 'Press'. During those times press was the 'mouthpiece' at a national and regional level. Bal Gangadhar Tilak started Kesari and Mahratta newspapers, Mahatma Gandhi founded Young India, and Harijan and Jawaharlal Nehru established National Herald.

In the current technological age, it is indeed great to see that the newspapers in India are still growing. More than thousands of newspapers are published daily in different languages in India and some of them are circulated widely across the country. Despite the birth of glamorous and fancier media that as electronics and internet media, the importance and value of print media have not been diluted to date.

Electronic media came into existence later, New media was introduced much later in comparison to the two previous media. Astonishingly at present New media reach and accessibility among media consumers grows indomitable in the media industry which leaves a deep fear among the masses that popular Print and electronic media might genre under 'traditional media' and become history in years to come.

Enter Caption

1.2. An Overview of the Media Industry in North-Eastern India

North-East India which is the prime focus of the study consist of eight states that is Assam, Arunachal Pradesh, Manipur, Mizoram, Meghalaya, Nagaland, Tripura, and Sikkim. Due to the geographical demography, North-Eastern India experiences the wave of journalism in later years as compared to the mainland states.

Assam was the first state to publish a newspaper among the North-Eastern states. Assam started its first newspaper published in 1846 with the launching of a journal called Arunodoi which lasted for over 36 years. After this, many newspapers have been published, to which some still survived to date and some disappeared in due course of time.

However, as far as print media is concerned in the state of Manipur, one among the North-Eastern States it is recorded that the indulgence of print media in the state started with the publication of the journal 'Meitei Chanu' during the year 1925-26. The journal edited by Hijam Irabot, who is considered to be the Raj Ram Mohan Roy of the state lasted for a very short period. In 1933 there was the publication of another paper called 'Dainik Manipur'. It was widely circulated even to the neighbouring state Assam. Mushrooming of the press in Manipur started after the state attained full-fledged statehood in 1972. People started to understand the importance the press held in building society by then.

The local newspapers in the North-Eastern region are witnessing rapid growth at present. There has been a swift increase in the number of newspapers in North-Eastern states. A present the eight North-Eastern states have a publication of multi-lingual newspapers in the region. The recent trends indicate that newspapers play a significant role in bringing changes in politics and society in the region. Despite the advancement of technology, circulation of the news happening in and around the North-Eastern states only among the eight states might show a probable reason that there can be a loophole in adapting objectivity, fair and unbiased style of reporting in other mainstream newspapers of India. Some of the presents circulated by local newspapers include Assam Tribune, The Sentinel, Eastern Chronicle, Nagaland Post, The Morung Express, The Sangai Express, and The People's Chronicle, etc.

As time brings changes, the North-Eastern states like other metropolitan states have joined the race in the media industry to establish private own news channels, Cable networks, FM radio, etc. The North-Eastern states have also experienced a bittersweet myopic vision of giant media while reporting for the North-Eastern states of India. New media is like the 'North Star' to people of North-eastern states, it is through OTT, personal blogs, etc., a whole new unseen before the sight of the North-eastern states is shown to the rest of the world.

Enter Caption

1.3. Reach and Accessibility of North Eastern news in the rest of the Indian states

According to Malcom X, *"The media's the most powerful entity on earth. They have the power to make the innocent guilty and to make the guilty innocent, and that's power. Because they control the minds of the masses"* his view on media draws a clarity on aspects of media capabilities.

There have been huge outcries from different sections of the North-Eastern states over the meager representation of the issues concerning the North-Eastern states in the mainstream media houses. Apart from the common issues relating to the insurgency and Armed Forces Special Powers Act in the northeast region, there are other valuable, newsworthy issues happening in the North-Eastern states. Yet, the Indian media often failed to uncover news concerning the northeast states.

Most of the time issues which took place in the North-Eastern states when unnoticed or were sometimes misrepresented to the larger population of the society. There is a communication gap between the North-Eastern states and the rest of the states. North-Eastern states being connected to the rest of the state by a narrow stretch of land which is commonly known as 'Chicken Neck' may be one of the reasons. However, this sole reason does not suffice the fact that the concerned states are fit to be barred from media isolation. "Mr. Subir Bhowmick, who was the first speaker, told that North East was never there on the media map. More people from the North East in the media industry could not ensure better and wider coverage of this region in the media. He informed that stories filed by reporters and journalists on Northeast are often rejected by editors" (Shambhu Ghatak, 2011, 11th Media Dialogue).

2. RESEARCH PROBLEM

Many times, the giant Indian newspapers and Television channels wealthily covered articles about the latest fashions, celebrity gossip, and the release of new movies or book reviews when there is a lot more worthy news happening beyond the realms of metropolitan states. It may be recalled that after the Guwahati molestation case made it to national news, the then Chief Minister of Assam Tarun Gogoi said "the national media tended projecting an only negative image of the north-east" (The Hindu, July 22, 2012).

The envelope of communication gap germinated between the North-Eastern states and the mainland states due to poor coverage and misrepresentation of news from the region. The obsession of national dailies in emphasizing news reports catering to insurgency and violence engraved the readers' minds with 'negativity' about North-Eastern states. Because media is

Enter Caption

the mirror of the society and simultaneously coverage of mostly militancy and violence in the North-Eastern states has sabotaged the image of the North-Eastern region. For example, Assam is known as the state of floods and the United Liberation Front of Assam (ULFA); most of the news concerning Nagaland is of the talks between the two fractions NSCN (Issac-Muivah) and NSCN (Khaplang); as far as Manipur is concerned, it is all about bandhs, strikes, AFSPA, and ambushes.

The myopic visions of Indian media have limited themselves and drawn a line to cover news not beyond violent events in the North-Eastern states. The underlying fact is that North-Eastern states have their uniqueness with their picturesque land, a place with large attractions of tourists; the states with rich cultures and multiple ethnicities are worthy to give coverage ironically, the decent insights of these states remain alienated.

Considering the factual significance of media in society as a medium to 'inform', 'educate', and 'aware' the masses, the inadequate 'space' of representation given to the mainstream media creates gravity of dissatisfaction amongst the people from the North-Eastern region.

2.1. RATIONALE OF THE STUDY

Most of the Indian dailies newspapers firms, TV channels, and radio broadcasters deployed a handful of journalists in the vast North-Eastern states, and some wholly rely on news agencies. Such lackadaisical attitudes of the media organizations can be one reason behind the coverage of insufficient news about North-Eastern states. Technically, it would be an impossible task for one man/woman to keep an eye on all the eight North-Eastern states. Accordingly, many issues despite their weightage to get published in the newspapers or broadcasted on TV and radio often overlooked and neglected.

The unparallel geographical locations between the giant media organizations and North-Eastern states may be a probable reason to consider 'proximity' while covering the region and this reason might result in Indian media slipping the attention from the North-Eastern states. However, this does not justify the fact that the North-Eastern states are overlooked in the Indian media.

This research study seeks to investigate the issues of coverage of North-Eastern News in Indian media, whether the coverage of news for North Eastern states is given importance with changing times or the Indian media continues to shut their eyes in regards to news related to the region. This research study will try to find trends of representation behavior and weightage given to the issues concerning the North-Eastern states in Indian media.

Enter Caption

3. OBJECTIVES OF THE STUDY

The main objective of this research is to analyze the coverage of North-Eastern news and its trends of representation in Indian media. The following specific objectives have been framed for this research study.

1. To find out if there are inclusions of North-Eastern issues on front pages of national dailies and primetime news broadcasts of Indian newspapers and TV channels.
2. To identify the beats that are preferred for reportage of Northeastern issues in Indian media.
3. To study the trends of representation of North Eastern news in Indian media over a specific period.

4. RESEARCH QUESTIONS

To meet the purposed of the study, the following research questions arise:

1. Do the Indian media (National dailies, News Channel both Radio and TV) give coverage for North Eastern issues on front pages and prime time?
2. What are the beats that are emphasized in reporting North Eastern issues in Indian media?
3. What are the trends of representation of North Eastern news in Indian media?

5. REVIEW OF LITERATURE

Newspapers one among the oldest media has important role in educating and disseminating knowledge to the masses with its daily updates on current affairs and social happening in and around the globe. In order to maintain credibility various media persons, remain vigil to cover news happening around. How far the media can be the 'watchdogs' to the North-Eastern states is something to be disused.

There is a rich source of research studies and analysis conducted in relates to coverage of North-Eastern states in Indian media written by people form walks of life including research scholars, journalist and social activists.

Sen. (2011) speculates that North-Eastern India remains behind a veil of selective silence for the rest of the country and the world. The involvement of Northern news in mainstream media is minimal. This fact becomes even more apparent when compared to the extensive coverage of the events in the rest of the country. According to the findings of the comparison, voices from the North-Eastern states receive very little space in newspapers and even less

Enter Caption

airtime on privately owned television news channels that are printed or broadcast from metropolitan areas such as New Delhi, Bombay, Bangalore, Chennai, or Calcutta. This study also discovered that "often, North-Eastern coverage remains trapped in stereotypes." With its conflicts, tribes, and underdevelopment, this is India's area of darkness, an area of little interest to the media, those in charge of governance, and the country as a whole. The dominant image of the North-East in metropolitan India remains that of a wild frontier" (ibid).

According to Saha (2015), the relationship is exacerbated by a "lack of focus and limited reporting of the region in mainstream newspapers." Thakur and De (2015) discovered that issues from Delhi, Uttar Pradesh, and Maharashtra are given ample space in national English dailies. Northern states such as Gujarat, Rajasthan, and Jammu Kashmir are frequently mentioned in the national media. Following up news stories are also carried out in some Indian metropolitan states such as Delhi and Mumbai. Similarly, news stories from the South are adequately covered. However, in the media channel scenario, North-Eastern India is one of the least important. According to the study, "Nagaland lynching is the only issue that came on radar among all the issues in the North-Eastern states." As a result of this incident, Assam's home ministry issued a high alert, and both national and regional media outlets covered the story. Only conflict-related issues are addressed in media representation of the North-Eastern region. Thus, the media of this democratic nation almost entirely ignores an important part of the nation, as if they have no role in nation building and no place on the country's map. As a frontier region with a shared international border, the region has been subjected to numerous onslaughts of the independence war. They suffered greatly prior to independence as a result of colonial rule, and they continue to suffer after independence as a result of the total avoidance by the social sectors, including administrators and the media, of issues that could aid in the formation of opinion and consensus on various relevant and distinguished issues relating to different ethnic groups and their specific needs and desires."

According to Bhutia (2012), the national media has a callous attitude toward the coverage of North-Eastern states. "The north-eastern region of the country receives insignificant space and time in national newspapers and on television channels." The reason for such an attitude can be found in Herman and Noam Chomsky's book "Manufacturing Consent," in which it is described how "money and power are able to filter out the news fit to print." . There are at least 200 ethnic minority groups in north-east India. These organisations have nothing to do

Enter Caption

with the commodities manufactured by multinational corporations that advertise in such media. Naturally, these ethnic groups have little clout in our national media" (ibid).

Palchoudhury. (2015) discovered that when Manipur was on the verge of facing a 68-day economic blockade, none of the mainstream media took the slightest interest in covering the story. Only after 68 days of economic blockade did the media awaken from their long slumber. "National channels and national dailies did not see the need to cover this significant event." Under the banner "Is Manipur part of a mainland India?" CNN-IBN hosted a panel discussion on the economic blockade. The most remarkable aspect of the story is that the Editor-in-Chief of CNN-IBN had to persuade his producer for this panel discussion, who asked him a surprising question: "Why do you want a panel discussion on Manipur?" This question itself reflects the attitude of mainstream media towards India's alienated child" (ibid).

6. RESEARCH DESIGN

To get the result of this research study following methodology is applied. Using this selected methodology, the conclusions are deduced which will be seen in the later section of this research study.

6.1. DATA COLLECTION METHOD

The study used an online questionnaire survey method for data collection. This online questionnaire survey consists of a 111 (one hundred and eleven) sample size. The online questionnaire survey contained 2 sections, the first section consists of 14 close-ended questions and 1 open-ended question, and the second section is all about the demographic details of the respondent. The respondent participated in the online survey through the process of Snowball sampling method.

The responses gathered using collected data from the online survey are analyzed quantitatively. The online questionnaire survey is conducted among media consumers who have access to any form of Indian media namely daily English Newspapers, Television, Radio, and New media. Survey information is obtained through electronic devices such as laptops and Mobile phones. Since the survey is conducted online, the respondents belong from different states of India. The online survey was accessible and allow to participate to an individual who falls under the age range of 18 to 60 above.

SELECTION OF TIME FRAME

The research study covered the following time frame:

Enter Caption

1. 2000 to 2005
2. 2006 to 2011
3. 2012 to 2016
4. 2017 to Present

Selection of Unit of Analysis

The unit of analysis for the study of this research paper are news articles, breaking news, and features.

7. ANALYSIS

Media Access:

The online questionnaire survey was participated by 111 numbers of respondents from all over the country. The data collected shows that 53.2% of respondents access Newspapers and Television as their source of infotainment, 79.3% a whopping number of respondents are inclined to New media (Internet) to keep themselves updated with happening around. Whilst Radio and other media cater to small numbers of respondents i.e., 27% and 10.8 % respective. Though India has the second-largest print market in the world, the cited figure is evident that Indian audience/ media consumers are evolving with changing times. Perhaps, there is a need to analyze further to see whether a change has been brought amongst Indian media also while covering North Eastern news, and not misrepresented, judgemental, minimal or no coverage news of this region.

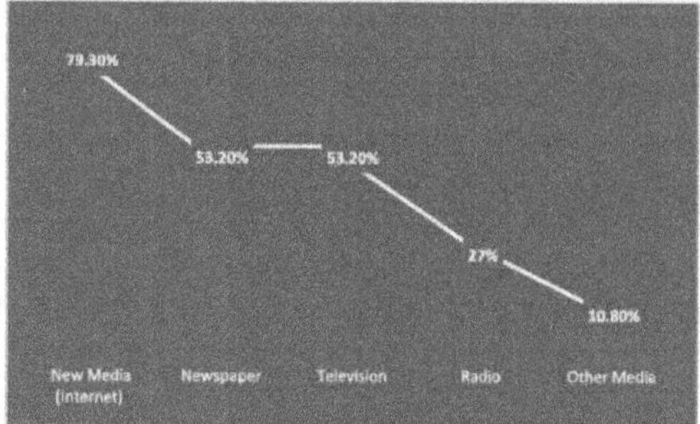

Figure: Media Access among respondents

Enter Caption

Demographic detail:

The online questionnaire survey is conducted keeping in mind the vast geographical distribution of India. To gather unbiased, genuine opinions the online survey does not give focus on only one or two states rather participation in the online survey is made by respondents from all over the country. The Snowball sampling method is utilized to gather responses to the survey. The following table shows the number of respondents from each state.

Sl.No.	Name of State/City	No. of respondent
1	Assam	2
2	Arunachal Pradesh	3
3	Bihar	10
4	Gujarat	5
5	Haryana	5
6	Jharkhand	2
7	Karnataka	9
8	Kerala	5
9	Ladakh	3
10	Madhya Pradesh	3
11	Manipur	18
12	Maharashtra	3
13	Mizoram	7
14	Orissa	2
15	Telangana	3
16	Uttar Pradesh	10
17	West Bengal	8

Awareness of North Eastern Region:

In an online survey conducted, when enquiring about their consciousness of the North-Eastern region, it is found that about 89.2% are aware of the region. However, despite being the fact that people lavishly enjoy many technologies wonderment with better access to information in comparison to a few decades ago still about 9% of the sample size found to be completely ignorant of the North-Eastern region and the remaining 2% choose to be in dilemma state of mind. The data collected from the online survey found that 62.2% watch, listen to, and read news on daily basis, out of the total number of respondents about 45.9% watch/ listen to prime-time news on Television and Radio. Refer to the graphs given below will give a better understanding of the details.

Enter Caption

Enter Caption

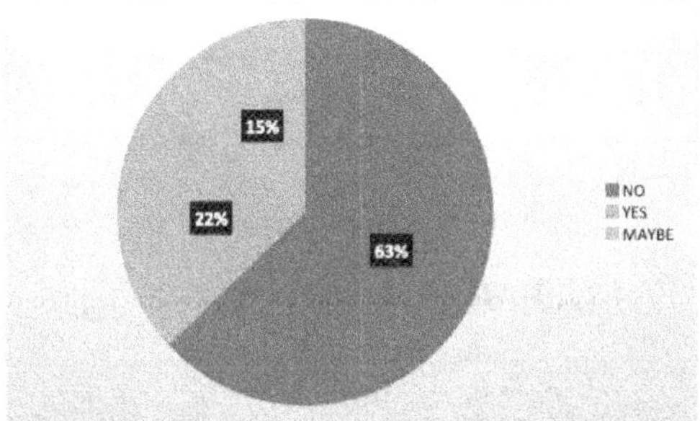

Graph: Coverage of NE states news or any report in Indian Media

The graph above depicts that 63% of the respondents state that there is no coverage of North Eastern states in Indian media. About 22% agree that there is coverage of NE states news in Indian media and 15% of the total sample size is between half and half. Percentage of disagreement to coverage of North Eastern states news scored highest of all three-opinion provided in the questionnaire. The quantitative results of these particular questions show that the news from NE states is not provided with enough space in Indian media.

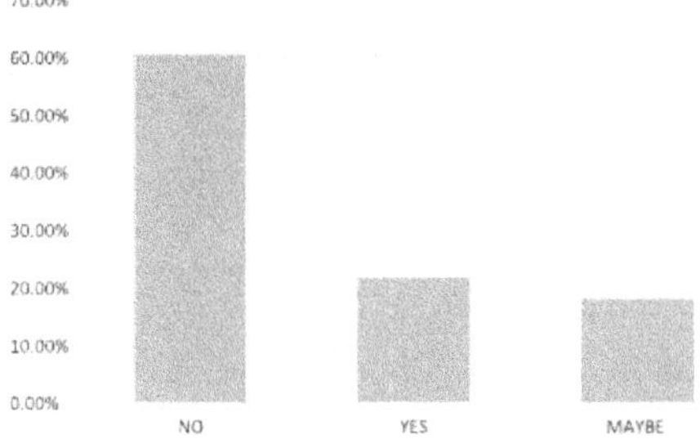

Graph: Coverage of NE region news on the front page of major Indian Newspapers

The above graph shows that 60.40% agree that there is no coverage of North Eastern region news on the front pages of major Indian newspapers. 21.60 % stated that there is a

Enter Caption

publication of NE region news on the front pages of a major Indian newspaper. The historic achievement of Hima Das in 2018 was not newsworthy enough to get coverage on the front pages of Indian newspapers. The major newspapers in India did cover Hima Das news in the sports section unfortunately, the success journey story of Hima Das which could be an epitome to provoke many athletes in the future did not dominate the newspaper that day. Meanwhile, attention was poured on Wimbledon and the big Indian game "Cricket".

North-Eastern region news did not either do surprisingly well in case of news broadcasted during prime time. The results of the survey remain the same that is 60.40%, 21.60%, and 18 % of respondents disagree, agree, and remain in between the option respectively in terms of broadcasting news of the NE region in prime-time news on both Television and Radio.

Enter Caption

News genre exposed to media consumers:

It is seen from the previous research study of others that there is minimal coverage of the NE region in Indian media. The researcher fears that considering the sample size, focusing on one page of newspapers or one-time slot news broadcasted for the day on Television and Radio might not draw any results. Henceforth, the online questionnaire survey gives leverage to the respondents to respond to the survey considering the multiple pages of newspapers and time slot of the news broadcasted.

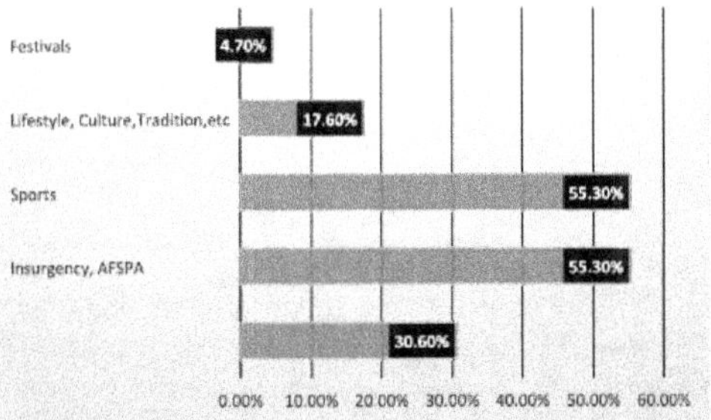

Graph: NE news genre respondents find common

The graph above depicts some of the common news beats the respondents come across regarding North Eastern news in Indian media. 55.30 % of the news about the North-Eastern region is about Insurgency, Armed Forces Special Power Act (AFSPA), and Sports. The remaining 30% caters to crime stories happening in North Eastern Region. 17% of the news reported are about lifestyle, culture, and tradition, and a handful of 4.70% reports about festivals of the North Eastern Region. North-East states consist of 145 different tribal communities, each tribe has its own unique culture and festivals. Yet, it is ironic that hardly a few populations are aware of the festivals and traditions of North-East states.

Trends and Representation:

To study the trends and representation of NE states over time in Indian media, a certain period is chosen for this research study. The graph below will provide the details of the study.

Enter Caption

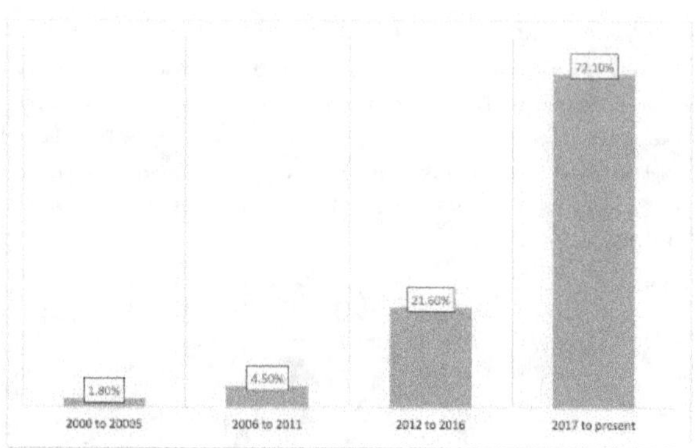

Graph: Period showing a representation of NE states in Indian media

The data gathered through the survey shows 72.1 % of respondents agreed that in the above given period i.e., 2017 to present show maximum representation of the North-Eastern region in Indian media. From the 2012 to 2016 time period reports of North Eastern states are included in Indian media and about 21.6 % of the respondents agree with it. However, in early 2000 very few coverages of the region are done.

The research study also finds out that respondents are not satisfied with the present news beats given the emphasis to cover about North-Eastern region. Hence, in open-ended questionaries, respondents have opined their views on which they desire the Indian media to focus on while disseminating reports for North-Eastern states. The table below will give a gist of those beats media consumers expect Indian media to include in their reportage.

Sl.no	News Beat respondent expects Indian media to include while coverage of NE Region	Number of respondents
1	Business news	04
2	Crime news	08
3	Cultural news	22
4	Developmental news	16
5	Education sector news	05
6	Human Interest	03
7	Lifestyle	15
8	Political news	04
9	Social issues news	14
10	Sports news	09

Enter Caption

Note: Overall number of online questionnaire survey respondents = 111
Total no. of responses to this open-ended question = 100

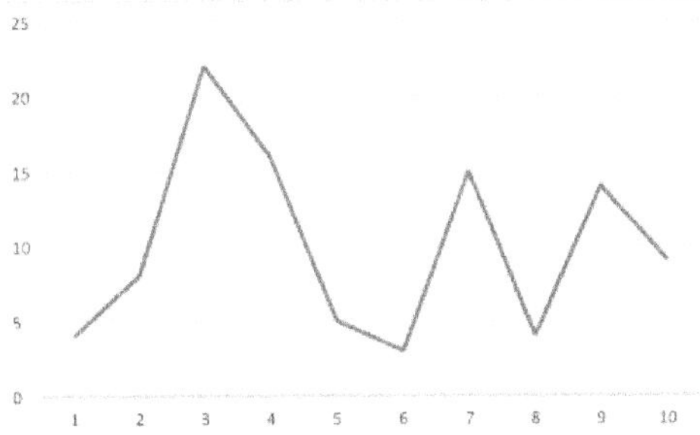

Graphical representation of the above table

The graphical representation of the above table is the testament of media consumers which shows that Cultural, lifestyle, and social issues beat picked highest orderly. The data portrayed media consumers' opinions on which beats they want to read or see in regards to North-East states. The survey results are antithetical to what Indian media have been feeding to the audience all these years.

Conclusion:

The online survey sample size is considerably pea-sized in juxtaposed to the actual population of India which is 1.38 billion people. Despite its pea-sized sample holding almost 10% of people ignorant about the North Eastern region evidently can be related that the number of the people unaware of the region will increase with an increase in sample size. In such a situation media is the torchbearer in connecting, mending gaps, making aware of the unknown facts about the region to the rest of the states.

India is considered the second-largest Print market in the world adding to which Indian Radio broadcasting service reaches out to millions of listeners even in the remotest area of the country. Astonishingly, the survey data shows that 80.2% of respondents read and listen to news about North Eastern news via the Internet medium, about 20.7% of respondents read about the NE region in Newspapers, just 16.2% watch about NE region in Television medium

Enter Caption

and only 2.7% heard in Radio which is satirical considering reach and accessibility of Radio medium.

Although there is an increase in trends of representation from 2017 to the present, the fact positive news like human interest, lifestyle, education, etc does not get enough space in Indian media, camouflages the lackadaisical, imbalance attitude of Indian media. 72.1% of the online survey responded that Indian media coverage of North Eastern news is unsatisfying, the half-cooked report is undesirable and media consumers expect more inclusions of the region.

Proximity can be one of the many barriers to media incompetency to report little details of the North East states. However, major events like natural disasters, achievements, or representations by people from North East in historic events are justified and should be given enough space and treated fairly while reporting.

Media reports must consider fair and balanced reporting seriously. Misinformed, misrepresented reports can sabotage the image of the people from this region. After all, media is a powerful tool that embraced people to see the way they want to be seen through its weapon of lens and pen.

Many events are occurring beyond the realms of crime and insurgency in NE states. For example, the vibrant Yak dance of Arunachal Pradesh, the popular, colourful, and full of life Hornbill festival of Nagaland, the meticulously and synchronously choreograph eye-pleasing bamboo dance of Mizoram, an anecdote of 'Ras Lila of Manipur are few events which will be worthy of exposure and acknowledgment to the rest of the people.

Trends of representation of North Eastern state news have slightly improved in the current scenario in comparison to the early 2000s. Nonetheless, the coverage of North Eastern region news is primarily reported in New media. Cybermedia is in its infant stage, especially in a country like India, such media mediums have lesser reach and accessibility in judgment to Print and Electronic media. The NE region already is facing a crisis with misrepresentation and limited reporting to these two later media. Perhaps, representational trends will gain good results when all the three media Print, Electronic, and Cybermedia contribute equal space and time and are not treated differently.

Enter Caption

REFERENCES

Sen, A. (2011). Marginal on the map: hidden wars and and hidden media in North-Eastern India. *Reuters Institutes for the Study of Journalism.*

Reetu, (2014). Dear Media, why no coverage to floods in north eastern India? *Oneindia.*

Akoijam, I. (2013). Coverage of the north east declines. *Inbooks.*

Bhaumik , S. (2015). Forgotten floods: why India can't afford to ignore Assam. *BBC News.*

Sengupta, A. (2007). North-Eastern India: through the prism of the national media. *Institute of Peace and Conflict Study (IPCS).*

Chongloi, H. (2017). Portrayal of North-Eastern India in mainstream media a case of underrepresentation and misinterpretation. *International Journal of Research in Social Sciences,* ISSN: 2249-2496.

Bordoloi, P. (2014). Mass media in north east India: the trends of conflict reporting. *Openindia.*

Bhutia, U. (2012). Media must revisit north- east. *In media practice.*

Sharma, I. A. (2011). Origin of journalism in north- east India. *MediaWatch*

Mukhim, P. (2018). Hey mainstream media, Biplab Deb isn't the only news in North-Eastern. *TheQuint.*

Batra, A. (2013). Vivid: is North-Eastern ignored by media. *exchange4media.*

Singh, S. R. (2007). The role of media in north- east. *E- pao*

Mukhopadhyay, S. (2015). Militancy and combat: The AFSPA and media coverage. *Global Media Journal – Indian Edition.* Sponsored by the University of Calcutta/www.caluniv.ac.in. ISSN 2249 – 5835 Summer& Winter Joint Issue/June- December 2015/Vol. 6/No. 1& 2.

Pregu, Kr. U . (2014). Media Coverage on Ethnic Conflict in North-East India: An Analysis on the Issues and Challenges in Conflict Communication. *Global Journal of Finance and Management.* ISSN 0975-6477 Volume 6, Number 1 (2014), pp. 89-92.

Enter Caption

Media Representation of North-East India: A Print Media analysis Souvik Acharya and Anjani Kumar Jha:

Introduction

Media is the fourth pillar of our democracy. In a country like India, the role of media in the society as the watchdog of our democracy is very crucial indeed. Communication is taking place all the time in each and every corner of the word. For proper communication to take place a particular model is followed. The message emanates from the source and travels through a medium and finally reaches the destination or receiver. Proper feedback from the receiver means the message is properly delivered and the communication has been taken place successfully. For a proper communication to take place, the necessity of the medium is necessary. When the message travels from a source to a huge number of receivers or audience then it becomes Mass Communication. For proper Mass Communication to take place, again the role of media becomes important. The day to day different news all around our society reaches to us through the media. In earlier times there were folk media through which different messages reached the people. Folk Media included different forms of traditional ways of conveying important social messages to the audiences. Later, the different forms of media emerged from Print media that is newspapers and magazines, to radio, then television and the present day internet and digital media. News comes to all the masses through news media which include newspapers that is print media, television news channels, and todays different convergent digital media means. It is very important for the News Media to work properly with objectivity, balance and fairness which are the basic founding principles of journalism. Biasness should be avoided at all costs so that proper news which is fair, balanced and objective is presented to the audiences. The media houses should keep in mind that their main target should be to serve the society not making profit only.

Fairness, Balance and Objectivity in Reporting

News is one of the most important things, which the common masses and people get daily through different news media be it print newspapers, radio or television news. For transferring of information from one place to the other a proper medium is always necessary for the dissemination of the message. In the same manner what is happening all around us in the society in different fields like social, political, sports, economics, and foreign affairs can reach us only through the news media. The media is aptly called the fourth pillar of our democracy, as it helps and performs the role of watchdog of our democracy. Since the early days of news media, one of the basic principles of reporting and journalism are objectivity, fairness and balance in the news they are presenting. There should be objective news, that is subjectivity or biasness or opinioned news must be avoided, though it has been into different parts of the practice in the recent times. Many media houses are run by big media oligarchies or owners who have different vested interests, and accordingly the editorial policies are also made. Editorial policies affect the balance, fairness and objectivity and leads to the news presentation in a certain way. This ultimately affects the principles of journalism and reporting. Political inclination towards certain parties or even some news houses are directly or indirectly controlled by political parties and leaders and this again leads to the biasness in news presentation. News should be presented in accurate details and objective in nature. Lakhs of readers and viewers depends on this news about different issues of the society. In our democracy it is obviously the role of the fourth pillar that is the media to maintain its neutral stand and focus on service to the nation and its audience.

North-East India and its representation in Indian Media

India is always a country of unity in its diversity. India is always united by its different cultures which are varied in nature. From Kashmir to Kanyakumari, from Gujrat to Assam, India is stretched in all directions. Each place has its unique social, political, historical, cultural and economic history and background. The North Eastern Part of India which consists of the states of Assam, Arunachal Pradesh, Manipur, Meghalaya, Mizoram, Nagaland, Tripura and Sikkim also. The first seven states are also known as the seven sister states of India, together with Sikkim they form what we call "North-East India." These states have their social, political, historical and cultural backgrounds. They have many similarities amongst themselves in all the fields, and share common bonding among each other. Indian news media covers different issues related to all parts of India, still it can be said that like every other part of the nation, the north eastern part is not covered in that much aspect. From the beginning only, specific news stories related to terrorism, conflicts, inter-tribal and ethnic clashes are what mostly reported from these parts of the country. Mostly, negative, violence, sensational news is covered from this north eastern part of the country. There may be many reasons behind it. Though number of positive news stories happen in these parts of the country as well covering education, health, development , sports , personal achievement and many more. But still we can find the news media covering only negative news stories related to protests, conflicts, terrorism and the likes. TRP and profits may be one of the foremost reasons behind news coverage of this kind. Firstly, the news houses be it newspapers and television channels all run on the main task of making profit generation and also focus on areas and their news from where their main sources of revenue generate. North East always remains on the fringe news stories which fill up the pages of the newspapers if we consider print media. As discussed terrorism and conflict find its place regarding north east India, but the many positive and development stories are very rarely covered. Also, another factor as in the main areas like Delhi, Mumbai, Kolkata, Chennai have different news reporters and journalists associated with different organizations. But when it comes to north east India, many news houses only have few reporters assigned covering huge parts of the states. It becomes impossible for them to cover the vast areas of different states of north east. Thus many news stories do not reach the newspaper headlines and remains unnoticed from the Indians. Looking at the future it must be said that as new India as shaping each day, the Indians are much more connected to each other, they also want to be connected to the North Eastern part of the country, and vice versa. Thus one of the most important roles to be played is by the media in covering news related to North East India and acting as a bridge between North East and rest of India.

Rationale of the Study

This research study is conducted with the main focus to cover North East India and the print media coverage of issues related to North East India. Many research studies and surveys are carried out in relation with media and newspapers that is print media, but very little focus is given to media coverage of issues related to North East India, Thus the main focus and aim of this study is to bridge this gap and find out North East India finds its place in the coverage of News Items related to print media that is newspapers. It is very significant study because newspapers the backbone of our democracy and society, and how it covers issues and places from different parts of the country and different cultures including the North East is of very importance.

Objectives

1. To find out the pattern of news coverage by print media on issues related to North East India.

2. To find out the reasons why print media covers marginal amount of news related to North East India compared to other parts of India.

Research Questions

1. What is the news coverage pattern of print media on issues and events related to the North East India?

2. Why the media including print covers news and events related to North East India very less and marginally as compared to other parts of the country?

Research Methodology

This research study is conducted with the main focus of North East India. This study focuses on how the print media and media in general cover the news and events related to North East India. The researcher uses mixed methods of qualitative and quantitative methods in this research. The study uses content analysis methods in collecting and analyzing data from different primary as well as secondary sources. The research also conducts focus group discussion and interviews among few news readers and journalists to assess their views on North East India and media representation of this area.

Analysis and Findings

In this research study four print media editions of Times of India, The Indian Express, Hindustan Times and the Hindu, all New Delhi editions were taken for content analysis. The data found out are put in the following tabular form and the details are analyzed along with. For analysis the February month 2022 was taken as time frame and within this month these four newspapers and their content on North East India was analyzed.

Print Media Representation and News Media Coverage of N-E India

Newspaper	Types of Content Coverage
The Times of India	Sports News- 11; Conflict/Crime News- 24; Political News- 15; . Development News- 4; Social and Cultural News- 6; Arts & Entertainment News- 5; Total News on N-E: 65.
The Hindu	Sports News- 8 ; Conflict/Crime News- 16; Political News-12 ; Development News- 4; Social and Cultural News- 5; Arts & Entertainment News- 4; Total News On N-E: 49.
Hindustan Times	Sports News- 12; Conflict/Crime News-17 ; Political News- 14; Development News- 5; Social and Cultural News- 8; Arts & Entertainment News- 6; Total News On N-E: 62.
The Indian Express	Sports News- 8; Conflict/Crime News-15 ; Political News- 12; Development News- 6; Social and Cultural News-3 ; Arts & Entertainment News- 4; Total News On N-E: 48;

News Media coverage of Northeast News

Analysis of the Print Media News Coverage
The Times of India

As we can see, in the month of February, the figures to the left hand side tells the story of news coverage of Times of India ,about the news coverage on topics related to North East India. The Times of India is one of the most circulated and read newspapers in India among English dailies. The study found out in the month of February, it covers total 65 news stories on the entire North East India on different topics. As it is evident North East covers entire seven sister states and Sikkim, that is a total of eight states , but leading English daily covers only 65 news stories in the entire month. Now the following figures depict the pattern of news coverage by this daily. In the sports section, and news related to sports the daily covered 11 news stories out of the total 65 news stories and news related to conflict and crime top the list with 24 news stories. Sports are a positive side of the news which spreads positivity amongst the youth and the society more emphasis should be given on this segment. While crime or conflict news numbered 24 out of 65 and this is huge. Though this kind of negative news will only spread negativity about the area, still the readers who live in other parts of the country are bombarded with news related to these kinds. Politics is indeed a very important part of our society and news related to political events are indeed very important. This leading daily also likewise covered 15 political news stories related to North east India out of the 64 stories. Now if we come to the other parts including development, social and cultural, arts and entertainment, the respective news stories covered are 4, 6and 5 respectively. This is a crucial area. The majority of the readers in India gets attached and interested to an area by news of these three topics, like development including health, education, then social and cultural and news, arts and entertainment news But this daily covers very less amount of news stories of North East India on these topics, and this pattern must be changed for the betterment of the society itself.

The Hindu

The Hindu is one of the oldest newspapers in India. It tends to cover news on different topics and different parts of the country. In the analysis we can find put that the total number of news stories in the month of February by the Hindu. The total number of news covered were 49 out of which majority 16 news stories were on conflict or crime. 12 news stories on political. This pattern again makes it clear that major print media gives emphasis mainly on news on politics, conflicts and crime on North East. The news on sports numbered 8 out of 49 which is very less if the youth of the society is concerned who are very much enthusiastic and interested about sports topics. The rest of the news stories on development, socio-cultural and arts and entertainment numbers very less 4, 5 and 4 respectively. Among Important print media like the Hindu which have considerable reach among its readers and help in the decision making process must put a thought that is a total of 49 stories in the entire month enough for covering 8 states. The pattern should be given importance and more news on uncovered topics should be included.

The Hindustan Times

The February month Hindustan Times covers still more amount of news stories on the different states of the North East. It covers 62 total numbers of stories on the North East. It again remains a matter of concern that news on development is 5, on social and cultural topics is 8, arts and entertainment is 6. These are the areas which connects the interests of the readers to these North Eastern states be it Assam or Arunachal Pradesh. But, the number of news stories remains so less that it is not fruitful. Political news numbered 14, conflict and crime topped the list with 17 stories and sports included 12 news stories.

The Indian Express

The Indian Express in the month of February covered lesser number of news stories numbering 48, out of which the chunk of news stories were on conflict and crime numbering 15, political news numbering 12, sports news numbering 8, development news were 6 in number out of 48. The rest social-cultural and arts and entertainment were 3 and 4 in number respectively. It again must be mentioned here that readers' interest always on positive news like arts, entertainment, social cultural, sports and these kind of news stories must be more in numbers. Yes sensational news of crime, conflict and politics may fetch circulation on temporary basis, but developmental news will build the future of the society.

Findings from focus group discussion with Newspaper Readers

The research study conducted focus group discussions with ten persons who are active newspaper readers and tried to find out how the different kinds of presentation of news stories in the print media affect them.

Q.1. What is the impact of news stories about North East India in print media?

Response: This question was actively discussed and moderated among the ten participants, all of whom are avid news readers of the print media. The majority of them are of the common opinion that in print media that is the newspapers; very less number of news stories is covered on North

East and so likewise the impact it makes on readers is also very less. Since eight different states are covered under North East, but compared to that the news stories make very little impact upon the readers.

Q.2.Which kind of News Stories are mostly found in the newspapers about North East India?

Response: Print media indeed play a very important role in the minds of the readers. News on different topics and different areas are covered on the newspapers which are read by its readers. All the respondents were very much vocal in this discussion regarding this question. Their main topic was the maximum number of news they find about north east India are either conflict related, or covers crime , maybe terrorism of the armed militants in the North Eastern states, or ethnic clashes in the states of North East. Sometimes different political news also find the places, but other kind of news find very little place. These were the observations of the panelists in the discussions.

Q.3. What do you think are the reasons North East India are not finding its places in the newspapers which it deserves?

Response: The respondents or panelists of the discussions gave their valuable and crucial responses on this topic. The discussion was very fruitful and important regarding to this question. Many find the fact that policy of the newspapers may be not that much tilted towards the North East, and very little importance is given to this part while news coverage. Another fact that came out in the discussion is that profit from the news coverage of this region is marginal compared to other parts of India, for this reason a local news of Delhi or Mumbai finds importance than those in Assam , Manipur or Meghalaya. One more point that came out in the discussion is that the number of reporters or newspersons covering the North Eastern states is much less than that of the other parts. Likely for one or two persons to cover entire parts becomes impossible and only few important news makes it to the headlines.

Q.4. What should be the pattern of news coverage and depiction of North East India in the newspapers of India?

Response: This was one of the most important questions discussed among the respondents and many important points were observed by the researcher. Some of the following describes them. Importance must be given to different kinds of developmental news related to health, education system, which should be brought to the limelight according to the arguments of the panelists of the discussions. Secondly, more positive news related to sports, culture, social and traditional festivals of these regions including lifestyle and achievements of different personalities should be covered by the print media. More number of the news reporters and journalists should be appointed in the North Eastern states, so that proper news coverage can be done.

Findings from Interviews with Journalists

Journalists are the backbone of our society, they bring to us news from different interior parts of the country. They become the voice of the millions through their news reporting and writings on different issues throughout the country. For this research study a group of ten journalists associated with different organizations were interviewed telephonically on conference and their combined responses were observed and recorded by the researcher. The researcher provided with open ended questions on which their open discussions took place in the interviews. The responses are recorded in the following manner.

On being asked about the relation between news coverage and policy of the newspaper houses, the journalists gave their opinions. Seven of them were of the opinion that policy of course directly impacts how and what kind of news is covered by journalists in the North East. They admitted that sensational news including terrorism, conflicts, ethnic clashes, political clashes, crime find more importance than other positive developmental stories related to North East. Since these kind of news stories help to gain advertisements and other circulations they make it to the headlines according to the journalists.

On being asked whether it becomes possible for the journalists to cover wide range of news in different parts of the states, their clear and majority response was that, very less number of correspondents are deputed even by big houses to the North Eastern belt. And likely, many news stories remain uncovered, and the owners and editors also find it less important to cover wide range of news on North East. Even according to the journalists, if different kinds of news from these places are not brought to the readers, how can the millions of Indian readers connect themselves with the North East and vice versa.

On the issue of news coverage pattern of the newspaper houses, the journalists opine that yes change must be brought in the news coverage pattern. More fresh, positive and developmental news should be done on the areas of the North East. In this manner the people of North East will also get a chance to connect to the mainland India. They will get a chance to present their cultures, traditions though the newspapers and print media, this change must be brought in by the news houses.

Journalist's opinion or sensational news is again disheartening. According to them also news which are sensational on topics of crime and conflict, insurgency and terrorism always find their places in the newspapers. It seems like North East is represented only by these negative news stories to the rest of India. But according to the journalists this is not the case. Many more news from local places, different events and festivals happen daily and they must be brought to the limelight and in this the role of journalists is most important is admitted by the respondents only.

Conclusion and Recommendations

North East India including the eight states of Assam, Arunachal Pradesh, Manipur, Meghalaya, Mizoram, Nagaland, Tripura and Sikkim is an important part of India. It must be stated that throughout the years since independence these areas have faced neglect from rest of the country. But with new India taking shape day by day, the scenario is changing. North East is day by day gaining importance in the socio political scenario of the country. Media always acts as the watchdog of our democracy. It presents different news related to different events in the society to the people. Likewise, when it comes to North East India, the role of media and especially newspapers that is print media is very important by large and far. A newspaper that is the print media acts the bridge in connecting the North East part of India and rest of the country. It Media under represents North East then there will be no one to take this role. So it is recommended that print media and newspapers must cover more events and news of North East India, and present them to the readers. Not only crime and conflicts, but daily local news about their daily problems, achievements, stories related to development of the region should be brought to the forefront. In this way it will be possible to connect India to its north east. Readers read numerous stories but rarely find stories related to North East. If more news about different issues on the North East is covered, the readers will also find interest and connect to the issues of this region. Many misconceptions are there among the Indians about the North East part of the country, but it's the duty of the fourth pillar of our democracy to remove all these misconceptions and bring North East to the front page stories of the newspapers, then only the society will give its importance to the North East India.

References

Arijit S (2013) Silent War and Silent Media: Reporting resistance in Northeast India. In: Miklian J, Kolas A (eds.) India's Human Security: Lost Debates, Forgotten People, Intractable Challenges, London: Routledgepp: 88-102.

Bahadur ST, Puthenpurakal J, Puykunnel SJ (2009) Christianity and Change in Northeast India. New Delhi: Concept Publishing.

Basnett, P. (2011). Coverage of Northeast India in the Indian Mainstream Media. *Artha Journal of Social Sciences, 10*(1), 12-18.

Chakrabarti P. A Study of Conventional Media Representations and Reporting of Violence in Assam.Global Media Journal 2018, 16:31.

Chongloi, H. (2017). Portrayal of northeast India in mainstream media: a case of underrepresentation and misinterpretation. *International Journal of Research in Social Sciences, 7*(5), 613-623.

Pegu, U.K. (2014).Media Coverage on Ethnic Conflict in North-East India: An Analysison the Issues and Challenges in Conflict Communication. *Global Journal of Finance andManagement, 6*(1). 89-92

Rogers, E.M. (1997). A History of Communication Study. New York: The Free Press

Roy, S. K., & Student, F. M. P. (2017). A STUDY OF NEWS CONTENT ABOUT NORTH-EAST REGION OF INDIA IN NEWSPAPERS PUBLISHED FROM NATIONAL CAPITAL (DELHI). *IJRAR-International Journal of Research and Analytical Reviews (IJRAR)*, 4(2), 566-571.

Sen, A. (2011). Hidden wars and hidden media in northeast. Reuters *Institute for thestudy of Journalism.* Oxford: University of Oxford

Shyam T (2008) Media and Conflict Reporting in Asia. Singapore: AMIC.

CHAPTER FOUR

REPRESENTATION OF MEITEI PANGALS (MUSLIM MINORITIES) IN TELEVISION COVERAGE AND NEWSROOM IN MANIPUR

Ereda Lourembam

1.Introduction

1.1 Origin of Meitei Pangals

The exact origin of the Pangals remain disputed till now. Some scholars claimed that the muslims have settled in Manipur before the sixteenth century. However, according to CheitharolKumbaba which was the Royal Chronicleof the Meiteis, the origin of the Pangals can be traced back to early 17th century.During the fight for ascension to the throne of Manipur between Prince Sanongba and Prince Khagemba, the former requested the aid of the Cachar rulerDimashaPrataphil.The Cachar king knowing his forces would not be enough, in turn seeks out the help of Muhammad Nazir, the then Nawab of Tarif. Accordingly, the Nawab's forces were dispensed under the command of his brother, Muhammad Sani.

Subsequently, the Nawab's army conceded defeat and Prince Khagemba ascended the throne. The king allowed some of the soldiers to reside in the valleys ofthen kingdom of Manipur. After a short while, the Burmese kingdom invaded Manipur and King Khagemba requested the aid of the

Nawab's former soldiers to help him join the war against Burma. After achieving victory, the king being very impressed with the soldiers gave them the title of Pangal which literally translates into 'strength' in Meitei language. Furthermore, he also gave them Meitei women to marry.

Based on their skill and vocation, the king assigned them family titles to act as their 'sagei' or clan names like Phundreimayumfor the ones skilled in using 'Phundrei' or lathe and Phusammayum for the ones skilled in making pots. Some more assigned surnames are Chesam for the ones involved in making paper, Khutheibam for the ones skilled in handicraft and design, Korimayum for the ones skilled in making copper vessels, Phisabamamyum for the weavers and many more.Altogether, there are 77 clans that exist.

Lastly, King Khagemba also set up an administrative office called PangalShanglen or Mangkan Shang at Kangla and the principal head of the office was titled as Kazi who is tasked with handling the administrative as well as the judicial matters. And thus, the Pangalcommunity settled in permanently and regarded the kingdom of Kangleipak as their new homeland.

According to the 2011 census, the total population of Manipur was 28,55,794, out of which the Meiteis account for 41.39%, the Christian community accounts for 41.29% and the Pangal community accounts for 8.40%.

1.2 Cultural and Religious Significance

Slowly but surely, the Pangals assimilated to the local Meitei community's customs and traditions. The started to relish the local cuisine of Ngari which is fermented fish,uti, eromba, etc. When it comes to attire, they adopted the traditional garb of khudei for men and phanek for women. They also started using Meiteilon which is the language of the Meiteis as their mother-tongue. Their marriage ceremony was a fusion of Meitei rituals and the Islamic Nikah. Their houses were also constructed based on the style of Meitei houses.

All of these changes were incorporated without discarding their Islamic roots and identities which led to the birth of a new community called Meitei Pangals which we know of today.

1.3 Political Participation

Two Pangals by the name of Md. QaziWaliulla and Md. Basiruddin Ahmed were part of the committee in charge of drafting the constitution of Manipur in 1947. The latter was also inducted in the Interim Council formed after King Bodhachandra abolished the Manipur State Durbar. This was followed by four Pangals who were elected in the general legislative assembly elections.

One of the most notable political representatives from this community was Md. Alimuddin who held the post of Chief Minister from1972 to 1973. He was an exceptionally visioned leader who laid the foundation for many important institutes such as Manipur University, Regional Institute of Medical Sciences and Manipur Medical College. He also inaugurated the Manipur Public Service Commission, Law Commission and Board of Secondary Education.

Moving on to present day Manipur, the Stateconducted its 12th assembly election on 2022. There are a total of 60 assembly constituencies in Manipur and only 4 constituencies were contested by Muslim candidates. Out of which, 2 candidates were elected.

1.4 Socio-economic Status and Progressive Development

In a 2004 survey conducted by the Directorate of Economic and Statistic Department, Government of Manipur, the result showed that the Pangals were falling behind in comparison to other communities of the State. In terms of living condition, the situation was deplorable. Around 62 % were living in kuccha houses, 31.2% were living in semi-pucca houses and only a mere 6% were occupying pucca houses. Most of their living quarters do not have basic access to drinking water and poor to almost nonexistent drainage facility.

If we look at education, the literacy rate of Meitei Pangalswas 67.76% which is considerably lower than the state average of 76.94%.

When it comes to cracking the governmental exams like UPSC and MPSC, only a handful has successfully cleared it till date. In 2006, the State Government implemented a 4% reservation policy for Meitei Pangalswith regards to appointment for Government posts or services as well as admission to professional courses. This move did bear fruit and quite a few deserving candidates could fulfil their employment and education aspirations.

Unfortunately, majority of the Pangal population arestill living below poverty, being involved in the unorganized sector of manuallabor, masonry, construction, peddlers, street hawkers, etc. They live daily earning from hand to mouth with very limited access to proper resources.

1.5 Violence and Racial Discrimination

Ever since the settlement of the Pangals in Manipur, they have been living generally in peace and without any conflict with any of the other communities except for a major communal riot which took place in 1993 claiming 100 lives of Pangals and 4 Meiteis.

Cases of discrimination and racism have also been widely reported against them. Social stigma held by the dominant Meitei community and other non-Pangal community further aids to their marginalization. Due to their impoverished socio-economic background, most of them appear on news forrobbery and drug smuggling which leads to the perpetual stereotype of Pangals being associated as 'anti-social' and 'criminal' in nature.

1.6 Media Coverage and Portrayal on TV

There is no denying the significance media plays in building up a narrative for the audience to consume. At times, the people in charge of news collection and production tend to influence intentionally or unintentionally the narrative of the news. Journalists, reporters, editors, producers, etc. depending on their community might frame up the news favoring their own or giving it a communal touch even if it goes against their professional ethics.

When it comes to programs like news discourse, talk shows and panel discussions, they act as a platform for the common people to come forward and express their views.The guest who are invited range from political leaders, social activists, think tanks, educators, businessmen, legal and medical fraternity and concerned authorities of their respective fields. To reflect plurality and diversity, it is important to show equal representation from all communities encompassing the state when it comes to inviting speakers for such shows.

2. Literature Review

Since their settlement in Manipur, the Meitei Pangals have been part of the common fray of Manipur. Besides being the second largest religious minority in the State, they are included under the category of Other Backward Class. "They are a unique social constituent of Manipur society not only do they share in the economy and politics, but also represented in the unique culture of Manipur. Though they form a minority group, they occupy a unique position" (Salam, 2015).

Besides being marginalized, the Meitei pangals have always lagged behind other communities. Moreover, the state government have never properly heeded to any of their demands for economic betterment and social upliftment (Syed, 2018).

According to the socio-economic survey conducted by the Directorate of Minorities and Other Backward Classes, Government of Manipur on 2004, it was discovered that "Muslims lag behind other communities in all the indicators of socio-economic status" (Shah and Khan, 2019).

During the Pre-Independence era, "owing to the new system of administration, the British government had to introduce modern education in India to meet their pressing needs of commerce and economic activities by producing literate Indian manpower mainly for employment in clerical staff. As the British took little interest in the promotion of education among the masses, the new English education helped the better-off Brahmins leading to their entry into the high Government posts and occupations. The Meitei Pangals were left out of the new educational movement as they considered modern education as antagonistic to Islamic education and gave due importance to Islamic education. This deprived them of modern education, which in turn made them unqualified for employment, or to be professionals like lawyers, doctors, teachers, managers etc. and for working in the modern enterprises, state administrative machinery etc. MeiteiPangals continued a parallel education system based on theological education. Indigenous Madrasas were established in select places in the Manipur valley on individual initiatives where theological education was imparted in Urdu and Arabic. All these factors limited their participation in the new set-up of the economic system for a long time" (Khan, 2021).

Khan (2021) also pointed out that "the present occupational structure of the Meitei Pangals clearly reflects a high degree of backwardness prevailing in the community. Despite the various opportunities provided by the new economic growth, the Meitei Pangal occupational shift towards the sunrise sectors is not remarkable".

The Government of Manipur needs to muster up some attention for the appalling condition of the Pangal community's welfare. The number of officers can still be counted on fingertips. The reason for the backwardness of this community is to be blamed on the absent-mindedness of the authorities (Khan, Kadir&Rahman, 2015).

Media wields a heavy hand of influence and is often seen by the society as the only source of informalisation without much verification or fact checking (Ullah and Khan, 2020).

One notable characteristic of Indian news segment on television channels include debates, discussions and other argumentative style of programmes which deals in content ranging from serious political issues to social issues which affect the general populace (Alex, 2015).

In a report conducted by Oxfam India titled *Who Tells Our Stories Matter* discovered that many religious and ethnic minorities of the country are lacking severely in representation in the news content as well as in the production process of media houses.

The reasons for Pangal community's limited participation in media in general and in journalism in particular could be attributed to the low literacy rate of the community, lack of awareness of the importance of print media and the significance of newspapers, inability to sustain long financial constraints, lack of professionalism, non-acceptance of journalism as a profession, lack of professionally trained journalists among the Pangals,etc. (Khan,2021).

Many reasons can be given for conducting studies on the relationship of minorities and media. They are often disregarded in the sampling process so from a theoretical perspective, it is essential to analyze the minority group against the dominant group. Minorities are also part of the audience and have their own subjective preferences so it is crucial to study them. Lastly, from the society's point of view, minority inclusivity is crucial to solve existing prejudices which are racially and ethnically influenced (Poindexter and Stroman, 1979).

3. Research Objectives

This research attempts to:

- Analyzethe extent of representation of Meitei Pangal on Manipuri television media
- Access the level of diverseness and inclusivity in employee positions in Manipuri television channels
- Determine the role of television channels particularly talk shows and panel discussions for being a platform for Meitei Pangal to express their views

4. Research Methodology

Since the Meitei Pangal community predominantly resides in the valley region of Manipur, the two major TV channels operating in this region have been taken up. The TV channels are Impact TV and ISTV. Both the TV channels were kind enough to provide the employee roster with the relevant details of their respective post, ethnic/community group and religion.

In addition to this, the debate/panel discussion programs of both the channels were analyzed for a 3-month period from January to March 2022. The topic of the discussion as well as the ethnic/community background of the invited panelists were noted.

Lastly,a consensual survey was also conducted amongst the Pangal community. An online survey was distributed.Snowball sampling strategy was used whereby the first round of participants further disseminated the questionnaire in their own respective circles.

In total 40 respondents took part. The data collected had been codified into percentages and converted into charts and tables. They are provided below under analysis and findings.

5. Analysis and Findings

5.1 Impact TV Employee Diversity Analysis

Impact TV currently has 37 full time employees consisting of Chief Editor, Sub Editors, PCR Directors, Cameramen, Reporters and Video Editors and 17 contract employees consisting of News Anchors and News Correspondents. The community profile for both group of employees have been shown below (Ref.Fig.1 and Fig.2). There is zero percentage of Pangals in both.

Fig.1Fig.2

5.2 ISTV Employee Diversity Analysis

For its Imphal branch, there are a total of 101 employees where 86 are on full time basis and 15 are on casual basis. The employees consist of the Editors, Cameramen, Video Journalists, News Anchor and News Correspondents. The community profile for both group of employees have been shown below (Ref.Fig.3 and Fig.4). Again there is zero percentage of

Pangals in both.

Fig.3Fig.4

5.3 Impact TV Debate/Panel Discussion Analysis for the period of January to March 2022

Impact TV has a daily debate cum panel discussion program called ManungHutna 360 Degree Analysis. It is hosted by an anchor and runs for an average of 55 minutes. The topics of discussion usually centre on political matters, government policies, social issues, health and covid related subjects. The invited panellists include social scientists, civil society organizations, political candidates and spokespersons, academic professors, political analyst, activists, etc.

From January 2022 to March 2022, a total of 255 panellists were invited. The community profile of all the invited panellists have been depicted below (Ref.Fig.5). 242 panellists were Meiteis, 8 were Pangals and 5 were Tribal Christians.

Fig.5

5.4 ISTV Debate/Panel Discussion Analysis for the period of January to March 2022

ISTV also has a debate/panel discussion program known as Discussion Hour. This also airs daily for an average of 55 minutes. The discussion topics range from political and governance matters to social issues, local economy, environmental as well as health related subjects. Similar to Impact TV, the invited panellists include social scientists, civil society organizations, political candidates and spokespersons, academic professors, political analyst, activists, etc.

From January 2022 to March 2022, a total of 253 panellists were invited. The community profile of all the invited panellists have been depicted below (Ref.Fig.6). 240 panellists were Meiteis, 9 were Pangals and 4 were Tribal Christians.

Fig.6

5.5 Online Survey Findings

(i) Out of the 40 respondents, 45% belonged to 21-35 years of age, 37.5% belonged to 36-50 years of age, 12.5% belonged to 50 years of age and 5% belonged to 15-20 years of age.

(ii) In terms of occupation, 40.5% were government employees, 21.6% were students, 18.9% were self-employed, 13.5% were private employees and 5.4% were unemployed.

(iii) Upon being enquired whether they know of any Meitei Pangal who are employed as journalist or editor in Manipur, 51.3% responded yes and 48.7% responded no.

(iv) Regarding the number of times they have across Meitei Pangal being invited to debate/panel discussion shows on TV, 45% chose rarely, 37.5% chose occasionally, 15% chose never and 2.5% chose always.

(v) 65% of the respondents stated that there is an unequal representation of Meitei Pangal community in such shows while 35% stated otherwise.

(vi) 92.5% of the respondents stated that they wanted to see more of Meitei Pangal community being invited to such shows while 7.5% stated otherwise.

(vii) Whether such shows will play an important role as a platform for Meitei Pangal to express their views or opinions, 97.5% of the respondents chose yes and 2.5% chose no.

(viii) Regarding the existence of a preconceived bias or discrimination against the Pangal community by the other communities of Manipur, 61.5% of the respondents chose yes and 38.5% chose no.

(ix) Lastly, 65.8% of the respondents stated that Meitei Pangal do not have the same access to resources and opportunities as other communities in Manipur while 34.2% stated they do.

6. Conclusion

From the employee data of both the TV channels, it is clearly shown that there is zero percentage of Pangals amongst them. Majority of the journalists, editors, news correspondents, reporters and anchors come from the dominant Meitei community. This huge concentration of only one dominant community may lead to a biased or contorted reflection in collecting and presenting of news.

Even when it comes to the panellists who were invited to their discussion programmes, both the channels showcased more of Meitei guests than any other communities. The percentage of Pangals invited during the 3-month period was only 3% approximately of the total guests for both Impact TV as well as ISTV.

Pangals appeared a total of 17 times where 11 were either political candidates or party speakers, 3 were civil society members, 1 was a High Court advocate and 1 was a State Nodal Officer. The huge percentage of political related guests can be surmised due to the fact that Manipur was holding its 12th State Legislative Assembly on February 28th and March 5th. Hence, the entirety of January and February's share of discussion programs were completely focus on the election. This leaves a pertinent question whether any Pangal would have been invited at all if none of them contested in the election or came from a political background.

The data collected also indicates that social thinkers, poltical analyst, academic professors, doctors, civil society activists, etc. were only invited from the Meiteis. This can lead us to question whether there are any Pangals in Manipur, if at all who are holding such relevant posts and duties to be invited to such shows. Studies have shown us that the media content has a way of influencing the mindset of the audience. If such TV shows continue to only showcase the opinions and views of the guests belonging from the Meitei community, there is a chance of the Meitei community's perspective and views washing over the general narrative of the discussed topics. Minorities like Pangals would not be able to present their perspective on it. The survey that was conducted also claims that Pangals are in favour of seeing more guests from their own community be invited to such shows as there is an overwhelmingly unequal representation going on so far.

Media is a double-edged sword. If used correctly, it can do wonders for development and upliftment of the masses including the minorities. If used wrongly, it can only be a tool for gross under-representation and suppression of the minorities. TV programmes like debate shows and panel discussions are watched by many daily and these very shows will go a long way in being a platform for the minorities to express their voice.Knowing the weight of the importance they hold, they should stand true to their professional ethos and be more inclusive. They shouldreach out to more Pangalshailingfrom all walks of life to be guests for their programs. Pangals mostly come on the news for stealing and drug smuggling so in order to erase this stereotyped notion against them, inviting them on such shows will also be very fruitful. The Pangal community also professed on the survey that they are not getting the same access to resources and opportunities unlike other communities, so it will be crucial for them to use these shows to air their grievances as well. Truly, media has a very important role to fulfil in being the voice not just for the majority but for all.

REFERENCES

1. Shah, M. B., & Khan, Md. C. (2019). The State of Affairs of Pangal Women: A Feminist Perspective. *Feminist Research,* 3(1-2), 11-20. http://dx.doi.org/10.21523/gcj2

2. Syed, F. (2018). Reservation of Muslims in Manipur.*International Journal of Research in*

Social Sciences, 8(5), 242-251. http://www.ijmra.us

3. Khan, M. N. (2021). From warriors to journalists: Meitei Pangal occupational shift in history. *International Journal of Electrical Engineering and Technology (IJEET),* 12(3),25-34. DOI: 10.34218/IJEET.12.3.2021.004

4. Khan, Md. C., Kadir, Md. A.,&Rahman, Md. S. (2015). Status of Education among the Muslims of Manipur: Prospects and Challenges. *The Journal of Social Science Scholar, 2*(4), 96-109.

5. Salam, A. (2015). Political participation of Muslims in Manipur.*Shodhganga:*

A reservoir of Indian thesis. http://hdl.handle.net/10603/39535

6. Alex, R. (2015). The politics of representation in Indian media: implications of the portrayal

of Hindus and minority groups. *Westminster Research, University of Westminster.*http://www.westminster.ac.uk/research/ westminsterresearch

7. Poindexter, P. M., &Stroman, C. A. (1979, August 5-8). *Minorities and the Mass Media:*

A Review of the Literature, 1948-1978 [Conference presentation]. Association for Education

in Journalism 62dd, Houston, Texas.https://files.eric.ed.gov/fulltext/ ED176290.pdf

8. Ullah, R., & Khan, A. (2020). The Role of Mass Media in Shaping Public Opinion.*Research Gate.*

9. Oxfam India. (2019). *Who Tells our Stories Matters: Representation of Marginalised Caste Groups in Indian Newsrooms.*

10. (2019, November 09). Meitei Pangal's history retraced. *The Sangai Express.*http://e-pao.net/GP.asp?src=17..101119.nov19

11. Soibam, H. (2014, March 13). Marginalised within the margins: Meitei Muslims in Manipur.*News18.* https://www.news18.com/blogs/ india/soibam-haripriya/marginalised-within-the-margins-meitei-muslims-in-manipur-12912-748360.html

12. MMWO questions government on status of Meitei Pangal. *The Morning Bell.*https://themorningbell.in/mmwo-questions-government-on-status-of-meitei-pangal/

13. Ahmed, S. (2014). Manipur's First Chief Minister Md. Alimuddin remembered. *TwoCircles.net.* https://twocircles.net/2014nov21/ 1416545962.html

14. Raji, M. (2022). Muslims may play a decisive role in Manipur elections. *Awazthevoice.in.* https://www.awazthevoice.in/india-news/ muslims-may-play-a-decisive-role-in-manipur-elections-10013.html

15. Khan, Md. C. (2020). Reasons of the backwardness of Pangals in Manipur.*Mainstream Weekly.* https://www.mainstreamweekly.net/

article9984.html

16. Gurumayum, M. (2016). Muslims in the history of Manipur.*Imphal Times*.https://www.imphaltimes.com/it-articles/item/4582-muslims-in-the-history-of-manipur

17. Ahmed, S. (2013). Muslims offer prayers for those who killed in 1993 riot in Manipur. *TwoCircles.net*. http://twocircles.net/2013may05/muslims_offer_prayers_those_killed_1993_riot_manipur.html

18. Ali, B. L. (2020). Socio-economic importance of Meitei Pangal's 4% reservation in non-professional higher education to other communities & government.*Imphal Times*.https://www.imphaltimes.com/guest-column/item/19057-socio-economic-importance-of-meitei-pangal-s-4-reservation-in-non-professional-higher-education-to-other-communities-government

19. (2004, March 1-15). Socio-economic survey of Manipuri Muslims.*The Milli Gazette*.https://www.milligazette.com/Archives/2004/01-15Mar04-Print-Edition/0103200480.htm

20. Rizwan, M. (2010). Muslims in Manipur: A look at their socio-economic condition. *TwoCircles.net*.https://twocircles.net/2010jan11/muslims_manipur_look_their_socio_economic_condition.html

21. Malik, A. (2020). JNU Research Scholar accuses Mnaipur of harassing Pangal Muslims in newspaper article, state government responds with author's arrest. *Firstpost*.https://www.firstpost.com/india/jnu-research-scholar-accuses-manipur-of-harassing-pangal-muslims-in-newspaper-article-state-government-responds-with-authors-arrest-8257101.html

OTT PLATFORMS AND THE SENSORIUM ON THE SMARTPHONE SCREEN: NOTES FROM WOMEN'S PERSPECTIVES Aakriti Kohli

Introduction

The increasing popularity of the smartphone screen as a ubiquitous device points towards how it is at once an idea, media and technology, and our engagement with it in everyday experience has made it one of the dominant screens of our lives.The contemporary smartphone screen, in opposition to cinema, television, mobile phone, computer and laptop, signals towards new frameworks which determine the relationships between technologies, culture and individuals, and requires us to address the materiality and reality of these technologies and techno-cultures produced due to the transition into an individualised screen experience. The smartphone screen, unlike that of television and cinema is also more 'playful' and intimate in creating a personal visual and tactile sensory experience for the audience-user, thereby transforming the senses. Subsequently this study brings women's voices to the centre by probing the questions of screen cultures and screen sensorium produced, and the forms of engagement specifically with respect to the smartphone screen in contemporary times.

In an article published in *The Quartz* titled, "Indians love watching videos on their phones – as long as it is for free", an image of two men sharing a smartphone screen lying down on their beds, and another man lying down on a platform next to them using his smartphone as well, is deeply evocative (Bhattacharya, 2018). The article also cites a report published by the Boston Consulting Group in the year 2018, that one of the primary reasons for growth of OTT (Over-the-top) video platforms in India is the adoption of smartphones, followed by cheap mobile data and broadband.The central premise of the article was that Indians are gravitating towards using smartphones, primarily for watching videos, as long as they don't have to pay for them.

Rationale of the Study

In a study published by KPMG (2019) titled 'Unravelling the online digital video consumer' in 2019, about 87% of the respondents consumed online content on their smartphones. Spending 70 minutes a day on OTT platforms, every session was for an average of 40 minutes, and the viewing frequency was about 12.5 times per week. The study also mentioned that the age groups of 15-24 and 25-36 spend the most time per week at 9.2 hours and 8.3 hours respectively, though followed closely by the age groups of 37-50 and 50+ as well. Smartphones then are the most preferred medium to access OTT platforms versus a TV or a tablet due to its convenience and cheap mobile data prices by the youth.

The smartphone screen media has also generated new modalities of watching films and television content for audiences. OTT consumption on the smartphone screen displaces television viewing or watching films as a "family activity" in urban India thereby reconfiguring social formations (Mankekar, 1999). The inclusion of new content lexicon such as streaming and playing are reconfiguring the access and engagement with media texts on screen. With the access to this content mediated via the smartphone screen, across multiple platforms, there are newer ways of imagining the audiences as well. They no longer watch or tune-in, but stream content on devices, activating various modes of 'play'. They are more diverse in the content they consume but at the same time converge on few handful platforms available via screen media. Further, since research in media studies assumes an urban, English-speaking male audience, leaving out women's voices, perspectives and experiences, this study becomes important in its contribution to the study of the smartphone screen, sensuous and playful experiences and OTT consumption from young women's perspectives. Additionally since women's access to communication technologies is inequal, restricted and policed, it becomes imperative to unearth their perspectives on how they negotiate larger structures which impinge on their access to digital technologies.

Objectives and Research Questions

While the structural dynamics of OTT platforms, in terms of the content they produce and license, their marketing, distribution and publicity strategies, are influenced by their prospective audiences that are increasingly spending a significant part of their time online, it is also guided by the architecture of the smartphone screen, its interface, its functionality, its uses, its possibilities and limitations and its software. All of these aspects of OTT streaming platforms are crucial to understand (i) how the *screen sensorium* gets generated, activated and circulated in OTT spectatorship, one of the crucial questions of this study.

Secondly there are certain media experiences that cannot be neatly categorized as *consumption* or *use*, hence this paper questions (ii) if 'play' can become a productive term to think through consumption of media texts on the smartphone screen? Play can perhaps be used creatively to look at it as a mode of media consumption and as a cultural practice, specifically where there is *consumption* of new media forms not exclusively for instrumental *use* of digital technologies, which might be still considered ambiguous owning to their fleeting nature.

And finally, since research on media and communication technologies have hitherto assumed men as the default category in terms of user and audience, this study aims to specifically probe (iii) women's encounter with OTT consumption on the smartphone screen as a 'playful' experiences. Digital access and divide in our country remains unequal, operating on different levels of intersectionality – gender, class, age and caste, among others. In this sense this paper probes the gendered access to communication technologies and the creative strategies employed by women.

Review of Relevant Scholarly Debates

The contemporary smartphone screen, in opposition to the mobile phone, computer and laptop produces interaction via the senses - of touch, of vision, of space, and of hearing, enabling and making possible our experience of the screen itself. Sensing is the ability to perceive, and technologies increasingly help in configuring and enabling this perception, thereby ordering sensory experiences. Humans have historically amplified and extended their senses by using instruments and artefacts such as telescopes, microscopes, microphones etc. among other devices (Connor, 2005). In fact, it is not limited to these devices becoming routes for us to merely sense the world, but they also produce newer sensations and sensing capabilities themselves. Connor further suggests that the camera for instance knows how to 'see' on its own, and the microphone knows when it 'hears' a sound, acting and sensing independent of the subject. These technologies also adapt and become intelligent over time, adapting to their changing environment. The ability to sense then gets repositioned by technologies. The smartphone screen is a popular and widespread technology of sensation which directs us towards new sites and practices of sensation. While a lot of what the smartphone screen does is invisible and virtual, it simulates and stimulates our senses in how we navigate our everyday worlds. We now see (digital maps), hear (audio from it, and in it) and touch our phones. Our sensory taxonomies have been rearranged, in many ways augmenting the sense of sight, touch and sound, and extending it via light, location, mobility. Technologies play a significant role in the formation of sense. The touchscreen of the smartphone screens set it apart from other mediums such as that of the television or cinema. This tactile nature enables a kind of travelling through windows where you have to touch in order to see. The screen is held and cradled in the hand itself which is how the kinetic and haptic converge. This is the temporal collapsing of making and viewing images or "haptic experience of productivity" (Verhoeff 2012, p.84).Using the smartphone screen is at once a physical and performative activity. Unlike the viewing practices like that of television or cinema, it is not just consuming images, but of image-making constantly, it is production and reception at the same time. It also requires massive amount of coordination – between fingers, eye and hearing, screen and image, and space and time.

The social and cultural significance of the senses mediated via screen technologies reveals how sensuousness and embodiment get activated. There has been emerging sensuous scholarship, specifically with respect to understanding media texts. Howes (2003) defines Sensory Studies as a "cultural approach to the study of the senses and a sensory approach to the study of culture". The usefulness of this approach is that it recognizes the various subjective meanings attached to the senses. The study of auditory, haptic, kinesthetic and visual senses is crucial in my understanding of the screen mediated experiences. Howes and Classen (2014) in their introduction to *Ways of Sensing* emphasize on 'intersensoriality' or moving away from the traditional categorization of senses as independent to further the argument on the interplay between them. Marks (2002) in her work on multisensory media has advanced an approach of understanding art for instance, via multiple sensory approach. She expands on engaging with art through haptic perception and including kinesthetic and proprioceptive functions as well. She argues that artists for instance seek to interpellate the many senses of viewers by creating a multisensory experience which goes beyond the narrow confines of audio-visual aspects of a work of art. The field of contemporary sensory studies has examined a range of issues, for instance Sheller (2004) has studied how the marketing of automobile technologies involves the stimulation of very specific senses, Parisi (2008) has looked at the re-framing of the touch of sense in the context of video games, and Bull (2000) has examined the use of portable music-playing devices in urban public spaces and how it transforms the users' sonic experience of the city providing them with a private soundscape. Drysdale and Wong (2019) also provide a useful frame for conducting sensory ethnography by suggesting the development of a 'sensory sensibility' by making use of the role of senses in conducting research, being attentive to the senses and alert to the embodiment and expression of the same. Further they suggest being aware of the sensory capacities being utilized in everyday life and activities as a disposition during all levels of the research process, in order to study and understand the complexities and the emplacement of sensory experiences and expression.

Vannini et al (2012) in their work on sensual turn in sociology speak of how media and consumer culture rely on stimulating the senses and cater to the need for sensual pleasures through consumption of objects and services. Some of these pleasures are evoked via the powerful seduction of images, the commercialization of aromas and perfumes, the elevation of culinary tastes, and facilitated through modern technology - the commodification of touch and even satisfying our acoustic senses. Our everyday activities are getting amplified by appealing to our senses by the somatic work performed by media and consumer culture, screen media and technologies. Vannini et al make a compelling argument when they call for a "more-than-human approach to sensory studies" (2012, p.168) in order to adapt to the changing nature of the sensorium because neither technology nor biology solely determine our sensations and sensory experiences. They further elaborate on the approach that I have also followed that there is in fact an assemblage of actants (users, technologies, corporations, relations, developments, software, devices) that transform our sensorium and sensory experiences. They go on to argue that sensing the world or carrying out somatic work requires us to incorporate this dynamism of various factors in order to fully understand what makes our senses as well as the ways in which we come to sense the world. In that sense, the screen creates a particular kind of sensorium for the audience-user and hence if we "experience the world, others, and the self through our senses" (Gabriele 2008, p.240) then in the context of my study, the screen media and technologies further stimulate our sensory orientations in qualitatively different ways.

Classen (2012) in an introduction on the interpellation of our senses has discussed how the department store discovered and introduced sensory marketing by allowing customers to feel, touch and see products before buying them, as opposed to the practice of verbally asking for products to be retrieved by the salesperson in the store, for thereby engaging their senses fully. The experience of navigating OTT is much like the experience of visiting a departmental store then. There is stimulation of visual and tactile sensations. An audience-user is invited to, much like as in a store, to see, touch, open and experience audio-visual content with a flick of their finger. OTT on the smartphone screen, in comparison to cable television and cinema, offer the audience-user the sensory experience of visually engaging with content, of touching different library offerings by opening them, scrolling through them, and feeling this immersive experience sensually.

There is also considerable scholarship that has emerged with respect to streaming of content online, emergence of transnational television and transformations in cinema production and distribution practices. The consolidation and concentration by traditional big media corporations has also spurred fears of media imperialism, a frame that has been used by Fitzgerald (2019) for instance to study the globalised development of OTT video services as a new international communication order. This has also been explored by Cunningham and Craig (2020) in discussing media globalization and emerging patterns of distribution and consumption, making key distinctions between social media entertainment (SME) and professionally generated content (PGC) such as those by streaming platforms. Mikos (2020) has also mapped the emergence and form of the transnational television audience with the coming of global distribution platforms such as Netflix and Amazon. Netflix has also been at the centre of a sustained examination from various perspectives, including but not limited to, its business model and conception of spectators (Zundel 2014), its long-form programming and production practices (Jenner 2018) and unpacking of its recommendation algorithm (Frey 2021).

In signalling a "playful turn" Raessens (2014) has argued that play has not received a sustained examination within the field of media studies, apart from work on video games (which has been recent), to use it as a frame of analysis for other media forms and texts. The concept of gamification is also useful here in exploring the playful nature of media experience. Gamification refers to game like structures, rules and practices being deployed in non-game contexts to fuel user engagement and interest. Gamification is not entirely new but the contexts in which it is being adapted and adopted are certainly novel. The smartphone screen offers numerous possibilities for playful activities and communication. The concept of play is not only a characteristic of leisure, but can also be invoked in other contexts, such as that of consuming content interactively, and in this case, OTT applications.

Mapping Women as Screen Audience-users: Research Methodology

My interviews were held with young women between the ages of 18 and 30, residing in Delhi who self-identified themselves as 'middle-class'. I conducted in-depth unstructured interviews with respondents that were recruited from known networks between March 2020 to May 2021 via a time-bound open call for participation (Table 1). My respondents ranged from women who were studying and working to also those who identified themselves as homemakers. The interviews were largely semi-structured, informed by the following themes to address and speak to different theoretical and practical aspects of playful OTT screen experience enabling sensing: their viewing context and practices, bodily sensations and feelings emerging out of using the app, the change in how they use technology, functional experiences of using OTT, changes in lifestyle, social relationships and communication on social media, among others. In-depth interviews allowed for a thick description of women's experiences in relation to their smartphone screen usage, OTT consumption, and the 'playful' nature of this engagement. Wherever names are mentioned I have used pseudonyms in place of my respondent's names.

Screen Sensorium, Playful Consumption and Women: Analysis and Findings

The smartphone screen, unlike that of television and cinema is also more intimate in creating a personal visual and tactile sensory experience for the audience-user, thereby transforming the senses. Undoubtedly, the experience of going to the theatre is also a somatic one, with dim lighting in the beginning and complete darkness once the film starts, the temperature-controlled environment, plush seats and an overall cosy environment. For some respondents however, the chatter of fellow audience members, the crunching of the popcorn, among other things, either adds or subtracts from their experience.In similar ways, the watching of traditional television experience gets interrupted by advertisements, the movement of other people in the house, and sometimes even interruption by power outages or signal loss.Rama spoke at length about how the smartphone screen on the other hand offers a private soundscape, which eliminates distractions and ambient noise. The smartphone screen then has reconfigured the sensorium with the use of technologies to condition her bodily habits of media consumption.

"I mean we can use Bluetooth speakers with our television also, but when I use earphones with my smartphone screen, the audio feels more powerful, and the image even closer to me because it's in my hands, it creates a more personal and intimate watching experience. Sound effects feel more immediate and live with the earphones. Like I am less distracted because nothing else is there in my line of vision you know."

For my respondents, the smartphone screen is the default screen of their life, reading Twitter feeds and comments, reading blogs and even books on their phone, and the size of the screen not taking away but in fact redefining the idea of immersive play experience for them, making the screen more intimate, the content more private and personal, to the point that a private activity such as television and cinema watching can now be done in a public place. Subsequently since most smartphone screens now come with AMOLED displays (Active Matrix Organic Light Emitting Diodes), High Definition and even 4K resolution, and superior overall picture quality, that visual and aural intensity does not diminish for them.

The domestic context of viewing television and the theatre context of watching cinema earlier produced an associative sense of location. However with the mobility of the smartphone screen and uninterrupted mobile data, new sites of sensation get produced with consumption of content on the screen in other public and private viewing contexts. Watching content in public spaces leads to an interplay of different senses such as while commuting, waiting at the bus stop, in the class, in the mall as well as in private modes of consumption such as watching it in bed, under the covers, on the terrace, in the bathroom, etc. developing new kinds of perception and associations with media content. For Tanvi and Parishka, the emerging screen culture produces new sensitivities and new spaces of sensation thereby leading to the formation of new senses of association, proximity and immediacy.

"I don't know how this started, but I have gotten into this habit of watching a show or a clip while in the bathroom. Either I start a new episode, or continue from where I left, but I cannot do my business without watching something on my phone." - Tanvi

"My commute time to work is more than 2 hours. I watch all my favourite shows and films in the cab now. Earlier it felt weird but now I am no used to it that I look forward to my commute because I know I can watch it in a relaxed manner. Sometimes at signals people peer through the window curiously to see what I am watching, I would get ticked off earlier but not it does not matter to me." - Parishka

The sensing of the smartphone device also conditions the mediation of audience-user's experience with the screen. For instance the proximity sensor in smartphones, which is on top of the device, turns off the display when we are talking on the phone, when the phone comes near the user's ear, and turns on when it moves away. Further, inactivity on the screen leads to time-out of the display similarly. Some respondents spoke of how they would sleep while watching something on their phones, only to wake up and find that the screen has gone to sleep. Additionally the light sensor in smartphones adjusts the brightness of the screen by measuring the brightness on the user's face, thereby calibrating the most optimum light sensitivity for the audience-user. For instance, drawing a V sign to switch on the flashlight, or a circle to unlock the phone's camera, or drawing lines to play or pause music playback. Some smartphones also offer another gesture control whereby users can answer their phone calls by bringing the phone close to the ear. The Samsung Galaxy S5 phone has another feature called 'eye tracking', where the camera registers the user's eye movements, and will pause a video automatically if the user looks away from the phone.[19]Similarly in 2018 Apple introduced eye tracking and gaze control as part of its Attention Aware and Detection features in its iPhones, automatically dimming the screen brightness when the user looks away from the screen. As Richa says, the gesture sensors in the smartphones have similarly transformed her media consumption on the screen.

"When I watch something on my phone it is a very personal intimate experience and I have the power to choose what I want to watch, when I want to pause and when I want to stop. On television it feels very impersonal. Going to the theatre hall also feels like a community-experience, and with Covid who knows when and if we will ever go back. When I go on any app I can browse, read, choose, watch, stop and start again. I control it with my fingers or even just with my eye by not looking at the screen anymore."

The flip-side to this is also the visual fatigue of the OTT library display, with Shagunspeaking of the visual stimuli which can overload her senses with the problem of plenty, thereby producing sensory saturation. What Lipovestsky (2011) calls "hyperconsumption" in the era of hypermodernity, is the constant stream and play of new media and cultural commodities and services that enable constant consumption.

"Honestly sometimes my eyes start hurting, and it hurts to keep scrolling. Sometimes you just cannot choose what to watch, nothing seems exciting enough. Then I just get tired, either I keep the phone down or go on YouTube or maybe Instagram. But I do feel lost when deciding what to watch, because there is so much, and everything looks interesting, but not interesting enough to watch at that moment, so I just keep adding them to the watchlist."

Technologies not only amplify and extend human sensing capabilities, but also produce new sensations and sensing capabilities of their own. The smartphone screen has produced significantly different textures of media experience and consumption. Consuming televisual and cinematic content on the smartphone screen demonstrates how it is no more a social experience, but individuated, contingent and variable form of play. The smartphone screen has enabled our perception in an acutely different way, by ordering and configuring our sensory experiences. We have in many ways learnt the skill of how to sense with the smartphone screen. The smartphone screen and OTT has produced and adapted to the changing viewing practices. We have come to learn to sense via technologies, rearranging our sensory taxonomies. Anjali for instance shares how her sense of time or *chronoception* when it comes to watching content on her smartphone has changed. Due to the lack of any scheduling of content as with television time and cinema time, her time spent on their smartphone and OTT applications consuming content has become unhindered, interrupted only by calls or messages, or in some cases, heating up of the phone, and cramping of her hand and fingers.

"You know there is this new term called 'text claw', where your fingers clamp up and ache due to constant use of the phone. Like I feel my thumb sometimes starts hurting due to the constant scrolling. I mostly keep my phone cradled in my hand, and after some time you can feel the warmth of the phone due to the heat produced, and I immediately realise that I've been on the screen far too long (laughs)"

Increasingly there is a deeper relationship between our bodies and the external environment mediated by information communication technologies. Our bodies communicate data about itself to technologies, which make sense of this data and relay it back to us. The screen invites the user to have an interactive and immersive experience, offering possibilities of engagement far exceeding those of traditional television and cinema. Sujatashared her ability to do much more with the screen such as using touch to pause, take screenshots of certain scenes and uploading them on her social media accounts or sending to her friends, annotating it with her comments.

"I always associated watching a film in the theatre with family or friends.. Now I feel that sense of association does not exist, like I have new activities I do, like I take a screenshot and write something funny and post it online and send it to my friends.I think I'm very funny but my parents don't know that side of me. Once an aunt sent a screenshot of my Facebook post to my mother who was shocked that I spoke a certain language online. I blocked my aunt after that day."

Previously in the absence of the newly announced Digital Media Ethics code, most content on OTT platforms was streamed without censorship or certification, making use of the loopholes in the Cable Television Regulation Act and the Cinematograph Act. A proliferation of content with violence, drug use, profanity, sexual content was available for streaming without any restrictions. Indian television and programming rules for instance also adhered to time schedules for adult content.Shruti and Heena share how OTT then provides new kinds of viewing pleasures and sensations which were earlier restricted or not available to audiences(such as transnational content).

"We had become used to the fact that there will be no swearing on Indian television or even mention of sex for that matter. Even English films in the theatre would be censored. And imagine now you can watch anything at any time, without it being censored. You feel more connected to what you're watching when the characters are freely swearing in a situation where everyone

in real life actually does! And showing sex is not taboo anymore, it has really become normalised now because how can you censor the Internet. My folks get mad about the things I watch online, so now whenever they hover around I quickly swap screens." - Shruti

"My brother was always allowed to play very violent games when we were younger, but I was not allowed to by my parents. Now I really like the fact that there is no censorship when it comes to violence and action. As a genre it is so exciting. They don't treat us like kids who cannot watch blood, guns and death. It assumes that its audience is mature enough to sense what they are watching is fiction but at the same time be able to enjoy it also without random cuts."- Heena

The limits of time and scheduling constraints, television broadcasting rules of showing adult content (sexuality, violence and abusive language) late in the night for instance, and the interruption by advertisements, are irrelevant now. Sama for instance shared how she was keenly following the release of a Polish film, *365 Days*(Białowąs and Mandes, 2021), an erotic romantic drama, and was hoping to catch it in India, when Netflix offered it for streaming. Playing it on her smartphone screen at home gave her the privacy to watch the film away from the policing and prying eyes of her parents. Aditi and Ananya similarly shared how they now had the opportunity to consume erotic content on their smartphone screens in an increasingly mobile and private fashion.

" (Aditi)... Sexual content has become an integral part of OTT content, I mean it's so common no one is bothered even. I remember when Game of Thrones would air on Star World they would heavily censor it, cutting all sex scenes and beeping abuses, and the same episode on Hotstar would be free of censorship, obviously everyone ditched TV and watched Hotstar. It's thrilling to be able to watch such content without it being edited. And now there is hardly any show online without a sexual reference.... (Ananya).. Sometimes if I have to watch something very adult in nature, I prefer to do it on my phone because I don't want others at home to see what I am watching, because my Dad is very strict. I can safely read and watch what I want from the privacy of my phone screen."

The domestic experience of watching television and the sociality of cinema has now given way to individuated consumption on personal screens. Pooja shared how the domestic context of watching television at home earlier was dictated by parents or elder siblings.

"Usually my father or brother would decide what to watch on TV. Either it was news or sports or whatever my brother liked. It's not like I was not allowed to watch what I wanted but I could not dictate. Now it has been a long time since I watched television, because I watch everything on my phone. I share subscription of Netflix with 5 other friends because I cannot afford it on my own, and now I can watch whatever I want without my parents knowing."

Content is on-demand and instant, with new films being released online, and all episodes and seasons television series being available to audience-users. Many users shared how they feel relaxed as there is no urgency to watch something at a specific time, they know they can always go back to it. The sense of television and cinematic impermanence has been obliterated. Suniti shared that much like playing a game, with all the seasons and episodes available to watch at one go, it leads them to binge-watch more than a few episodes together, thereby producing a sense of living in the show's metaverse for some time.

"It happens that if I get hooked onto a show then I will watch many episodes together. I have noticed that because I spend 3-4 hours in a day on a show, I kind of start living in that world, in my head I sense I am still inside the show, constantly thinking about it. Obviously, that feeling doesn't stay for long, but it is there. And I remember talking about this with a few friends also who felt something similar."

There is however some level of technical frustration as well. Some respondents shared how buffering of content either due to their own slow internet connections or server issues with OTT platforms is frustrating, making them think about how television never buffered. The smartphone screen and fast internet speeds have further made stronger, the sense of immediacy and instantaneous nature of our interaction with technologies. Sudha revealed that when the screen hangs and becomes unresponsive, and the Internet disconnects, it immediately produces a sense of unease and frustration.

"SonyLiv is the worst app in the world, actually even ZEE5, it just hangs randomly, keeps buffering, if you try to zip ahead, it starts from the beginning, without explanation. And I get so frustrated sometimes I just want to throw my phone, because the phone just hangs you know, it's useless. I have to restart it and pray that SonyLiv is now in a good mood and behaves itself."

In many ways then the screen exists in and produces a multimedia sensorium, where the technology senses the user and in turn the user senses it through the screen. A very intuitive, real-time relationship between the screen and fingers and the palm develops, with streams of data flowing both ways.Sensory experiences show that the image on the screen can be expanded with fingers, pinched to a smaller size, disappear with a flick and appear again with a combination of finger gestures. The smartphone screen sensuously evokes activities of everyday life and hence calls for a study of the deep signification of sensation. Human interaction with smartphone devices via sensors for both incoming and outgoing information produces sensory experiences apart from the traditional five senses and there is invocation of other sensory experiences as well. The interaction between humans and smartphones is significant, because it's not just the stimulation of human senses but also the presence of mobile sensors themselves which together converge to produce specific OTT viewing experiences for instance.

The smartphone screen also lends itself very well to playful activity, because apart from being a communication device, it is also a playable device, one which we toy with when we are bored, for leisure and pleasure. The screen itself, and the apps within it offer unprecedented ways of pleasure to the audience-user . The concept of play on the smartphone screen with respect to media technologies, platforms and texts has the potential to complicate and even confuse the established silos in media and cultural studies, including but not limited to production/consumption, real/virtual, structure/agency, meaningful/banal, representation/simulation, to name a few.

In lieu of a Conclusion: Women's Streaming and Playing with the Screen

The smartphone screen, more than anything else, offers privacy and mobility to women in playing the content of their choice. It gives them the agency to choose for themselves what they want to consume. This element of choice and opportunity comes in a context where women's ability to choose, decide and access can be restricted for various reasons.

Additionally, the domestic context of viewing television and cinema has been displaced by a more private mode of viewing content, thereby freeing women from conditional access to communication technologies. Further as many of my respondents shared, the conventional assumptions about what women like to watch get dismantled in the context of OTT consumption on the smartphone screen. This is evident at four levels, first being that women can now play content they were earlier not allowed to access, second, they can now watch it privately without being embarrassed or being answerable to anyone, third, since for many young and old women economic independence is circumscribed by varying factors, availability of free content online is liberating, and finally it also allows them the opportunity to express their views about what they consume with their extended social network online.

With access to films and televisual content on the smartphone screen, modes of viewing have transformed, as have viewing practices, both temporally and spatially, a journey travelling from *tuning in* to *playing* content. A shift in perceptions of visuality has ensured that the exhibition context does not inflect the textuality of the content, and is not considered subordinate to it. Subsequently, the aesthetic and cultural assumptions of the intrinsic qualities of what television and cinema are, and are supposed to be, seem limiting, and even arrogant now, considering such ontological arguments do not seem tenable and viable any more, in terms of playing of content on the smartphone screen.

While consumption of OTT on the smartphone screen has not completely displaced television and the theatre, however the confluence of all video content on the smartphone screen has reconfigured screen cultures, constructing new viewing habits and shifting medium-specific preferences for audience-users. The push to hyperconsumption also drives them to pause content and search for commodities on e-commerce apps, inspired by what they are watching, thereby changing the modalities of media viewing and spurring spontaneous consumption. About 90% of my respondents shared that they solely use their smartphone screen for all their online shopping.

The concurrency of smartphone screen's ubiquity in human life at every time of the day and an intimate connection between users and their screens makes it a unique object of study. The screen in Marshall McLuhan's sense is literally an extension of humans, in a way in which our central nervous system is technologically extended by the screen – when users engage with the screen via multiple senses of touch, hearing and sight. Even our sense of space is affected by the screen, in our movement and positioning of our bodies, tilting of our heads, tracking out hands. The smartphone screen then is a sensuous form of capital, technology and media.

References

1. Bhattacharya, A. (2018, November 21). Indians love watching videos on their phones—as long as it's for free. The Quartz.https://qz.com/india/

1471445/indians-love-watching-videos-for-free-on-smartphones/

2. Classen, C. (2021) .*The Deepest Sense: A Cultural History of Touch.* Chicago: University of Illinois Press.

3. Connor, S. (2005).The Menagerie of the Senses.*The Senses and Society.* 1(1): 9–26.

4. Cunningham, S and Craig, D. (2020). Global Social Media Entertainment in *The Routledge Companion to Global Television*, edited by Shawn Shimpach, 49-59, New York: Routledge

5. Drysdale, K. and Wong, K. (2019).*Sensory Ethnography.*Sage.

6. Fitzgerald, S. (2019). Over-the-Top Video Services in India: Media Imperialism after Globalization.".*Media Industries.* 6:2

7. Gabriele, A. (2008). A Sense of Belonging and Exclusion: 'Touchability' and

8. 'Untouchability' in Tamil Nadu.*Ethnos.* 73: 523–543.

9. Howes, D. (2003). *Sensual Relations: Engaging the Senses in Culture and Social Theory*, Ann Arbor. MI: University of Michigan Press.

10. Howes, D, and Constance, C. (2014).*Ways of Sensing: Understanding the Senses in Society.* London: Routledge.

11. Jenner, M. (2014).*Netflix and the Re-invention of Television.* Cambridge, UK: Palgrave Macmillan.

1. KPMG. (2019). Unravelling the digital video consumer Looking through the viewer lens. https://assets.kpmg/content/dam/kpmg/in/pdf/ 2019/09/ott-digital-video-market-consumer-india.pdf

2. Lipovetsky, G. (2011). The Hyperconsumption Society in Karin Ekstrom and Kay Glans(eds) *Beyond the Consumption Bubble*. London: Routledge, pp – 25-36.

3. Mankekar, P. (1999). *Screening Culture, Viewing Politics: An Ethnography of Television, Womanhood, and Nation in Postcolonial India.* Duke University Press

4. Marks, L.(2002). *Touch: Sensory Theory and Multisensory Media.* University of Minnesota Press.

5. Mikos, L. (2020). Transnational Television Culture in *The Routledge Companion to Global Television*, edited by Shawn Shimpach, 74-83, New York: Routledge.

6. Parisi, D. (2008). Fingerbombing, or 'touching is good': the cultural construction of technologized touch. *The Senses & Society.* 3(3): 308–328.

7. Raessens, J. (2006). Playful Identities, or the Ludification of Culture. *Games and Culture.* 1(1): 52–57

8. Sheller, M. (2004). Automotive Emotions: Feeling the Car. *Theory, Culture & Society.* 21, no. 4–5 (2004): 221–42

9. Vannini, P., Dennis W., and Simon G. (2012).*The Senses in Self, Society and Culture.* London: Routledge.

10. Verhoeff, N. (2012). *Mobile Screens: The Visual Regime of Navigation.* Amsterdam University Press.

11. Zundel, J. (2019). TV IV's New Audience: Netflix's Business Model and Model Spectators in *Netflix at the Nexus: Content, Practice and Production in the Age of Streaming Television*, edited by Theo Plothe and Amber M. Buick, 13-26, Peter Lang.

EMERGING CORPORATE COMMUNICATION STRATEGIES AMONG CORPORATE FIRMS FOR ENSURING WOMEN FRIENDLY WORKSPACE DURING COVID Dr.K.S.Ragini

Introduction

Corporate social responsibility concept in corporate communication studies is a crucial and effective communication strategy to establish connection with the society, especially when the society needs it the most. Corporate firms and companies are viewing CSR concept not only as a strategy to enhance their reputation or promotion but also to cement better relationships with the society, making them socially accountable. Apart from providing financial assistance, the firms are trying to explore more effective communication strategies as part of CSR and trying to extend their community relations activities in order to establish their image among the public and to build a unique reputation among others.

Corporate firms with social responsibility initiatives can win the hearts of public, maintain a seamless relationship with the society and contribute to the developmental needs of the society .A firm involved in community relations can understand the needs and necessities of the society better and offer solutions to the problems of people. A business with social responsibility is the need of the hour prioritizing social, economic and environmental benefits. An employer with social responsibility adds to the value of an organization, morale and work ethics. A well planned, organized and structured corporate social responsibility team can contribute to the overall growth of an organization along with the development of society.

CSR concept has been widely discussed, practiced nowadays and has become a key component in the business strategy of organizations especially among IT firms. To be a part of society makes one socially accountable and responsible. CSR has thus become the central aspect of business and marketing communication strategy. Corporate citizenship enhances the corporate image and the corporate citizenship concept has to be reframed and revised in the post covid world for effective results and active involvement of firms in societal affairs. It invites customer satisfaction and more engaged employees that would result in better performance of firm as well as its employees. CSR in an organization allows conglomeration and partnerships with other firms, organizations, NGOs and government departments which provide a wider perspective to it and its wider application.

Gender and development is one of the key areas exercised and executed by corporate firms in their CSR communication strategies with at most interest. Women empowerment is viewed a very crucial concept to be attained at all spheres, especially in workspaces. Women have to be treated par with men and mental health of employees is important for the successful functioning of an organization.

Methodology

The study employs qualitative methods. Interviews with Corporate managers, HR managers and with the women employees of the firm were conducted to address the objectives of the study. Content analysis of Wipro corporate website was done to analyze the CSR reports during the year 2020-21, 2021-22 to assess their CSR efforts employed to promote working women during the pandemic. Interviews were conducted with corporate managers, HR managers and Public Relations officers ofWipro, a leading corporate firm regarding the CSR initiatives employed by the company during the last two years especially during pandemic promoting women employees' mental health in life, both in family and workspace.The study analyses the CSR activities carried out by the firm to fight mental stress during pandemicsituation among women employees, tries toanalyze the emotional health of working women during lockdown period, the challenges facedby them and other social responsibility measures implemented by the firm in this regard.15 corporate communication professionals were interviewed. Interviews were also conducted with the working 100 women employees in the firm .Content analysis method was also used to analyze and identify the gender friendly measures adopted by firm during the years 2020 – 21 and 2021- 22. Secondary data available on Wipro's website was also taken; an analysis of CSR reports published by the firm during the last two years was analyzed to find out the intensity of CSR communication, especially to analyze women friendly communication initiatives and strategies during the pandemic.

Analysis and Findings

Corporate social responsibility or corporate citizenship, an emerging field in the management research is viewed by corporate firms with utmost preference and importance. Wipro is a leading IT firm in India with a strong CSR policy and approach which has offered them a unique space among others. Corporate communication team at Wipro manages the communication effectively and constantly engages its employees in community relations campaigns and programmes. Interviews and analysis of annual CSR reports of Wipro reveals that the firm actively involves in social activities with strong CSR policy making them socially accountable.

During pandemic, the firm has taken special efforts to elaborate and revise the policies of CSR considering the crisis situation to be addressed. The Board committee revised the CSR plan to battle the Covid situation and was approved. Taking in to consideration the challenging times, it framed programs and policies to offer a helping hand to those struggling during pandemic situation. Social, political, economical, psychological condition of people during pandemic was researched and studied in depth and framed their CSR policies to offer solutions to the affected ones.

Corporate Social Responsibility team and its functions at Wipro

i. The team conducts meetings quarterly in a year and assesses its activities.
ii. The CSR board considers all the recommendations and proposals put forward by the members and take decisions regarding its implementation after consulting the management section of the firm.

Corporate Website and CSR Communication

Corporate website plays a crucial role in communicating CSR programs and initiatives. The corporate website has the following unique features, resulting in better CSR communication and well executed CSR projects. Need based experts group review CSR policies and make further revisions to meet the needs of the society. Features of CSR website includes:

- Fully functioning CSR website.
- CSR interactive features.
- Addresses community issues, issues related to environment, gender, educational concerns etc.
- Presentational features highlighting CSR activities.
- They provide feedback mechanisms and interaction space to public on their websites encouraging public participation.
- They make use of social media as an effective communication tool to reach people and to publicize their CSR efforts as social media is a great resource for CSR communication.

Confinement to home alone has increased the psychological distress among people, especially women which has led them to emotional stress. Women are facing extra burden due to harassments escalating behind closed doors. Incidences and reports of violence against women in households have also increased at an alarming rate says UN.The lockdown as a preventive measure against the Covid 19 pandemic has brought about a potentially far reaching, long term impact on people all around the world especially on women. The impact of lock down has adversely affected women and children who have become the worst sufferers during this period. Job insecurities and financial stress has further made the situation more painful that has resulted in the increase of stress among people. Social distancing, quarantine process and economic uncertainties have further fuelled anxiety among masses.

Mandatory stay at home rules has severely affected people, especially women and children. Both the employed women and domestic engineers are experiencing a similar situation during the lockdown days. Confinement to home alone has increased the psychological distress among people, especially women which has led them to emotional stress.Employed women are facing extra burden due to change in job nature that has changed to work from home Schedule plus the work they do for their family.

The study revealed that most of them faced emotional stress during lockdown days as they were restricted themselves or forced to be at home. Family issues were on rise, physical tortures; mental tortures were also reported by women in some households leading to domestic violence. Some of them expressed their anxiety as they do not know how to handle their children who were psychologically upset as they were denied entry to playgrounds or social places where they once gathered to share themselves.

Domains of Engagement

As part of their CSR activities, Wipro engages in a various sectors including health, education, gender initiatives, women empowerment, sanitation, environment, counseling, rural development projects, other societal development initiatives, gender development, business sustainability, primary health care, special policies for differently abled children, disaster management, rehabilitation projects etc. The firm also operates community development projects in co operation with government sector, NGOs and other social organizations. The company revised their CSR plan recently to meet the needs of society during pandemic. More inclusive developmental projects, rehabilitation schemes and effective crisis communication plans were framed to address the covid pandemic challenges.

Corporate Social Responsibility has a significant role in corporate communication sector especially during pandemic, as business, service organizations and global markets are strongly battling with the highly challenging time to establish themselves. CSR is a self-regulating business that offers public and its stakeholders a space to interact and participate at large for creating a scenario of being socially responsible and accountable.

Gender Initiatives

Lockdown has further put an additional pressure on working women as they have to work from home and do the additional responsibilities at home which has further caused mental agonies and psychological discomfort among them. Taking this in to consideration, Wipro has put forward employee friendly measures for work including work time reduction for women having children below two years. Interviews reveal that they have further initiated counseling sessions for women employees who face work load stress thus helping them in stress management. The employees also availed counseling sessions from supporting teams at Wipro on family matters including domestic violence cases which were on the rise during the lockdown period. Classes on gender rights and laws were imparted to its employees contributing to gender awareness and personality development that really benefitted its employees prioritizing gender equality.

Counseling Sessions

Respondents were of the opinion that sessions on psychological enhancement for employees, especially women employees, their children, sessionson gender equality, addressing domestic violence cases, stress management, awareness classes on homeVs work balance techniques, engaging and handling children at home during lockdown, work from home issues, sessions on encouraging vocational skills among children were conducted by the firm that helped them to gain and maintain psychological balance during stressful period.

Health care services

During pandemic, the firm could establish a unique position among other IT firms with its inclusive corporate social responsibility schemes. Wipro tried their maximum to reach its employees through various rehabilitation measures that helped many people and communities to overcome crisis. The firm arranged covid quarantine facilities, medicines, and health information campaigns. diagnostics of Corona cases, treatment to covid positive patients, assistance to health workers,health insurance schemes to employees, corona testing services, provided medical products, supplying hygiene kits, provided emergency health care equipments to government,mass testing campaigns, hand washing campaigns, sanitizing public places, distribution of surgical masks, sanitizers, surgical masks etc thus providing livelihood initiatives to its employees and people in this challenging times.

Online workshops and Training sessions

Wipro offered workshops and training sessions, medical camps on health care initiatives and encouraged its employees to participate actively in community health care projects and programs thus contributing to community development.

Revision of Policies

Wipro revised its policies to ensure work/life balance among employees, especially considering the stress of women employees and offered them flexible work shifts to ease stress balancing their personal and professional commitments, provided child care facilities, family friendly policies and childcare vouchers with a view of empowering women at work. Work from home policy was offered for all women employees.

Panel Discussions and Mentor Programs

The firm initiated and conducted special panel discussions and online mentorship programs regularly to make women voice their opinions, provided platforms to openly discuss the hardships they face at work during pandemic.

Evaluating Female Perception

Wipro provided several communication platforms and chances to help women speak up about their issues, encouraged their feedback and suggestions to evaluate their gender friendly policies at organization from the eyes of women employees.

Discussion and Conclusion

Effective CSR policy and proper implementation of CSR projects and schemes offer firms a unique reputation and branding strategy. Moreover it takes the firm to hearts of millions and also offers solutions to diversified problems and challenges existing in society. Though covid pandemic affected the corporate world immensely, the corporate industry tried their maximum to fight the crisis, retain business and to withstand the challenges of the pandemic. The findings of the study reveal that during pandemic, the firm tried its best to reach its employees, especially women employees executing more gender friendly measuresoffering solutions to their problems during the stressful period. CSR provided them a path to reach millions during crisis. Every organization has to review and restructure its CSR policies and strategies to meet the needs of the time especially during crisis situations. CSR Communication and other philanthropic activities by organizations have a crucial role to play during pandemic period. Dedicated and responsible CSR team is the need of the hour to establish and maintain a responsible and accountable etiquette among organizations.

References

Aguinis, H., &Glavas, A. (2012).*What we know and don't know about corporate social responsibility: A review and research agenda.*Journal of Management.

Argenti, P.A. (2003). *Identity, image, and reputation in corporate communication.* New York: McGraw Hill/Irwin.

Bernoff, J. and Li, C. (2008), Groundswell: *Winning in a World Transformed by Social Technologies*, Harvard Business Press, Boston.

Bowen, H. R. (1953). *Social responsibility of the businessman.* New York.: Harper Row.

Daft, R. L. (1997)..*Management* . Fort Worth: Dryden Press.

Fombrun, J. C. (1996). *Reputation: Realizing value from the corporate image.* Boston, MA: Harvard Business School Press.

Hargie&Tourish ,(2000) .*Handbook of Communication Audits for Organizations*, Routledge, London.

Holme, R., & Watts, P. (2000).*Corporate social responsibility: making good business sense.* Conches-Geneva, Switzerland: World Business Council for Sustainable Development.

Jamali, D., &Mirshak, R. (2007).*Corporate social responsibility (CSR): Theory and practice in a developing country context.*Journal of Business Ethics.

Maamoun, A. (2013). *Corporate Social Responsibility and the developing world: Commitment or duplicity?.*[Article].Business Studies Journal.

Werner (1995) .*Managing Company-wide Communication*, Chapman & Hall, London.

Yin, R. K. (1994).*Case study research: Design and method* (2 ed.). Thousand Oaks, California: Sage Publications.

CHAPTER SEVEN

A STUDY OF MEN PERCEPTION ON DAUNTLESS DEPICTION OF WOMEN IN INDIAN WEB SERIES Riya Maurya and Dr.Dheeraj Kumar

Introduction

India is among the biggest Internet market in the world. A large part of internet data comprises online video streaming. Due to the Covid19 pandemic, lockdown severed as a blessing for digital industries and OTT. Today,India is the fastest-growing OTT (over-the-top streaming) industry in the world and it is on the track to become the sixth-largest by 2020(Outlook, 2020). Aside from established OTT providers, the country's main broadcasters have also invested in the sector and launched their own OTT platforms. The emergence of the internet and OTT platforms boosted its growth and has covered a major portion of society because of its wide variety of content and easier convenience.(Sudhagoni et al., 2020).

The term "OTT" is an abbreviation for "over-the-top," which refers to audio-visual content delivered via existing TV receivers such as cables, satellite dishes, and set-top boxes(Urgelles, 2017). It is acontent delivery service that streams content over the internet. In this user can easily sign up or take subscriptions for services of various OTT platforms like Netflix or

Amazon Prime and these have a large repository of entertainment content from across the globe which can be accessed through different devices like phones, laptops, etc over the internet.

Digitalization and Globalization have paved a new way for media consumption. Rapid technological innovation and feasible internet connections have built better networking and delve intothe major scope of diverse content in India.

The Global Pandemic due to Covid 19 has brought many behavioral and lifestyle changes; social distancing and quarantine of people have increased digital consumptionat-home, which eventually result in an exponential rise in OTT consumption. According to KPMG Media and Entertainment Report 2018, after the US, India is expected to be the world's second-largest OTT market, with 45% estimated growth covering 138 billion by the end of fiscal year 2023.(Ravali, 2020)

New ideas and creative thought have given space

With the advent of the OTT platform, new ideas and thoughts have given space. Various small to high-level stories aregiven recognition along women who have been stereotyped as a soft, lovable, companions of the lead hero only is shifted more towards rough, hard, bold, even female actress is been only signed as the main lead in many Ott best web series.Examples of the Ott web series are***The Four More Shots, Illegal, Arya, Maharani, The Test Care and Human,*** *etc.*This transition is driven by more than simply economic need; it also necessitates some type of content evolution in mainstream and popular Indian cinema. OTT material is not only structurally distinct from Bollywood theatrical releases, but it has also played a key role in portraying a new, multi-layered view of gendered identities in India.(Joshi, 2020)

In the previous several years, streamers have had more female-centric programming and women at the helm of initiatives. "They have now woken up to the notion that women-oriented content sells," says trade expert Atul Mohan. We're not talking about your typical saas-bahukitch here. Last year, women played prominent roles in four of the ten most popular streaming shows. "It's only going to get greater," he says, citing prominent personalities like SwaraBhaskar, SushmitaSen, and KritiKulhari foraying into the field.(Mohanty, 2021)

People preference of OTT over other entertainment platform

More than half of North American maintaining online subscription of Netflix.Here are a few reasons why the format is preferable than traditional alternatives:

As Ott give high-value information at a low cost, streaming services are frequently seen as a cost-effective substitute for traditional cable packages.

Original content: In recent years, OTT firms such as Netflix and Amazon Prime have begun to create original content that is only available through their services. On platforms like HBO Max and Disney+, exclusive streaming rights for previously televised programmes are also available.

Many devices are compatible: OTT content is now available on a variety of devices. Any account holder can enjoy the same OTT experience from a game console, smartphone, tablet, or smart TV. This is the major demerit in traditional cable television.(Tapjoy, 2020)

Review of Literature

USER PERCEPTION TOWARDS OTT PLATFORMS (KERALA THRISSUR)

According to the study, maximum consumers have given neutral feedback against the video services of OTT platform. The future of OTT is also bright,because of their convenience and high-quality content, OTT services are popular among subscribers. Low-cost internet connection fees have also supported the growth of OTT services. People are excited when movies are released on OTT platforms at specified times, but they prefer to see movies in theatres rather than on OTT platforms. (Mohan, 2021)

THE STUDY ON PROFILES AND PREFERENCES OF OTTUSERS (INDIAN PERSPECTIVE)

According to the findings, consumers' profiles and tastes differ when it comes to content. It is difficult to say, that OTT will completely replace our traditional medium, despite large amount of money is been invested in OTT platform. Thus, it is reflected on the pricing strategy which is significantly very high. Internet was the major fuel for OTT platforms, so many telecom carriers are battling to compete with data plans in India owing to Jio, but the cost of OTT platforms has remained unchanged, so the average cost of customers accessing content on the platform has remained unchanged.

The study also shows there is a link between OTT platform subscription and social media usage. This means people are influenced by social media for choosing the content on OTT.

On OTT platforms, there is a correlation between age and content, i.e. content vary accordingly to the age.

Amazon Prime ranks top most platform for watching entertainment content, followed by Hotstar and Netflix.(Sudhagoni et al., 2020)

Women-oriented episodes, series, and films have been produced by a variety of OTTs in India. The Ott services includes Web Series like Aarya, Four More Shots Please!, Hundred, She, Flesh, and Bhaag. Madhuri Dixit, Beanie Bhaag Nene's untitled next project, as well as Bombay Begums, RaatAkeliHai, Choked, and Penguin, are now under development.(Mukherjee, 2020)

INDIAN WOMEN REPRESENTATION IN T.V AND FILMS

Women in the media: Women's roles in the media began in the 1960s, when television became a part of society. Women who appeared in newspapers, films, and television from that time onwards were given a lot of attention. The majority of media corporations were owned by giant MNCs and big businessmen who were all male. So, because they were unconcerned about women, they began to use them as a tool to attract viewers and enhance their ratings.(Ahmad, 2014)

OTT Consumption is higher among men as compared to Women

Male viewers have increased by twice as much as female viewers in recent years.

OTT platforms are most popular among the younger generation. The most OTT content is consumed by men between the ages of 15 and 30.

Women between the ages of 25 and 35 are the most likely to consume OTT content, and this number has risen over the pandemic. They produced less than half of overall consumption as compared to men. (Casino, 2021)

Objective

- To examine men's perception of Women as leading role in OTT shows.
- To identify men's views towards Women in Real Vs Reel life
- To analyse men views as OTT breaking the stereotype in depiction of women

Research Methodology

Instrument for the collection of data – The standardized questionnaire is used as an instrument to collect the data and it is a primary data of the research

Sampling method and technique: -Purposive Sampling isused, it is the Method of non-probability sampling. The questioner is made by considering these Demographic Variables Age, Gender, Qualification, etc.

Data analysis tools: - The tool to be used as correlational study for the analysis is SPSS Statistics software .

Population: The Respondents for this research is mainly men and those who watches OTT for their entertainment and the age group chosen is 18 - 55 +.

Profile of the users of OTT video platforms.

Variable	Attribute	Frequency	Percent (%)
Age	18-28	88	82.2
	29-38	14	13.1
	39-48	3	2.8
	49-58	2	1.9
	Total	107	100
Profession	Student	59	55.2
	Employee	44	41.1
	Businessmen	4	3.7
	Total	107	100
No. of OTT subscription	1	57	53.2
	2	26	24.3
	3	5	4.7
	More than 3	19	17.8
	Total	107	100
Most Preferable OTT Platform	Netflix	40	37.4
	Hotstar	27	25.2
	Amazon Prime	26	24.3
	Voot	2	1.9
	SonyLiv	3	2.8
	Zee5	3	2.8
	Other	6	5.6
	Total	107	100

Enter Caption

Table 1

Analysis: The above table shows, the descriptive characteristics of samples collected from the capital city of Uttar Pradesh, i.eLucknow.

The data shows the fond of OTT platform is more among the Youth, i.e age group between 18-28, i.e more involved in the Profession of Student and Employee. Also, the data shows people having at least one OTT subscription (53.2%) and the most preferable OTT platform is Netflix with (37.4%).

Correlation Analysis:

Relationship between Age Group of Men and Women Acting as Lead Role (OTT)

		Women Acting as Lead Role (OTT)	Age
Women Acting as Lead Role (OTT)	Pearson Correlation	1	.045
	Sig. (2-tailed)		.645
	N	108	108
Age	Pearson Correlation	.045	1
	Sig. (2-tailed)	.645	
	N	108	108

Enter Caption

Table 2: explained the result of the correlation between Age Group of Men and Women Acting as Lead Role (OTT). From the result, it is showed that Age Group of Men and Women Acting as Lead Role (OTT) are positively correlated to each other (0.045).

Thus, the stated Hypothesis is accepted, it shows positive relationshipbetweenAge Group of Men and Women Acting As Lead Role in (OTT)

H1: It shows a positive relationship between Age Group of Men and Women Acting As Lead Role in (OTT)

Relationship between the Women as lead character and acceptance of such character by men in reality

Correlations			
		Womenacting as lead Role	PrimaryRelation
Womenacting as lead Role	Pearson Correlation	1	.477[**]
	Sig. (2-tailed)		0.000
	N	108	108
PrimaryRelation	Pearson Correlation	.477[**]	1
	Sig. (2-tailed)	0.000	
	N	108	108
**. Correlation is significant at the 0.01 level (2-tailed).			

Enter Caption

• 87 •

Correlations				
		Womenacting as lead Role	TertiaryRelation	
Womenacting as lead Role	Pearson Correlation	1	.342**	
	Sig. (2-tailed)		0.000	
	N	108	108	
TertiaryRelation	Pearson Correlation	.342**	1	
	Sig. (2-tailed)	0.000		
	N	108	108	
**. Correlation is significant at the 0.01 level (2-tailed).				

Enter Caption

Correlations		Womenacting as lead Role	SecondaryRelation
Womenacting as lead Role	Pearson Correlation	1	.363[**]
	Sig. (2-tailed)		0.000
	N	108	108
SecondaryRelation	Pearson Correlation	.363[**]	1
	Sig. (2-tailed)	0.000	
	N	108	108
**. Correlation is significant at the 0.01 level (2-tailed).			

Enter Caption

Analysis: The relation in above table shows, the positive relation among Women as lead character and acceptance of such character by men in reality.

The Table 3.a shows Women as lead character and acceptance by men of such character in Primary relation, i.e. Wife, Girl Friend and sister is positively related i.e. (0.477).The P-value related with the correlation is below than 0.01

The Table 3.b shows Women as lead character and acceptance by men of such character in Secondary relation, i.e. in Society is positively related to among themselves (0.363).The P-value related with the correlation is below than 0.01

The Table 3.c shows Women as lead character and acceptance by men of such character in tertiary relation, i.e in Majority area is positively related to one another (0.342).The P-value related with the correlation is below than 0.01

The data also highlights the decline number (0.477).>(0.363) > (0.342), Men are more likely to have such boldness in primary relation and as the sphere increase men is like to be sure the acceptance of bold character of women in lager sphere.

Men preference as OTT breaking the stereotype in depiction of women

1=Strongly Agree, 2=Agree, 3=Neutral, 4=Disagree, 5=Strongly Disagree

Analysis: The data shows men are more likely to favour such Bold character in the OTT platforms with the 56 respondent, but in real life they prefer more Soft,Lovable women 57%.

Also, the data shows men tends to disagree with the statement that women has any negative impact of OTT or women are using their bold depiction in a negative way.

Findings and Discussion

- In todays era of internet, Majority of youth of age group (18-28) wit 82.2% are more inclined towards OTT, having at least one subscription i.e 53.3%.

- The most favourable OTT platform is Netflix with 37.4% are compared to others, with hindi as more favourable language 67.3%.

- Lockdown has brought more positive graph in the usage pattern of OTT, 43.9% people are watching OTT from last two years.

- More than half 68.2% prefer OTT for the entertainment than theatre, due to the quality of Content it has 57.9% and in content men mostly prefer Web Series 74.8%

Women Depiction in OTT and Men Preference

Men strongly agree with the statement that OTT has brought major change in the depiction of Women along they prefer dauntless depiction of

Women as lead character.

They life the shift in Women acting from the hero companion to rough and tough lead role.

But Majority of men, still in dilemma that Women could replace Men in terms of acting as lead role. They think it is neutral Women Cannot replace or can be!

Also, the correlational study shows that men are more likely to favour such depiction of women in reality. Men highly prefer such dauntless depiction of women in their Primary Relation i.e. Wife, Girlfriend and Sister. They also think and favour such depiction of women in Secondary Relation, i.e. society and even men being as majority of population also favour dauntless depiction of men by other men comprising acceptance by majority population.

The survey also shows that men totally disagree with the statement that OTT has any negative portrayal on women and alsothey are disagree with the statement that Women are exercising such dauntless depiction in a negative way.

Conclusion:

OTT platforms such as Netflix, Amazon Prime, and Hotstar, which are now among the most popular, are gaining popularity. Because of its content, OTT services are popular among men and they favour OTT for entertainment.

Men are extremely supportive of fearless depictions of women in entertainment platforms, according to the study, and they want such a transition in reality.

The user perception is measured using two variables by the researcher. The study discovered that such a character is accepted in all relationships.

Because the survey only included OTT users from Lucknow, generalizations for the entire country are inappropriate

References

Ahmad, F. (2014). Representation of women in tv and films in India. *Indian Streams Research Journal*, 4(4), 1–6. http://www.isrj.net/UploadedData/4658.pdf

Casino. (2021). *OTT viewership among male audiences increased two-fold compared to females: Study - BusinessToday*. https://www.businesstoday.in/latest/trends/story/ott-viewership-among-male-audiences-increased-two-fold-compared-to-females-study-316344-2021-12-21

Joshi, A. (2020). *How OTT in India Shifted Popular Representations of Masculinity.* https://www.filmcompanion.in/readers-articles/how-ott-in-india-shifted-popular-representations-of-masculinity-tvf-netflix/

McLeod, S. (2018). *Cognitive Dissonance Theory | Simply Psychology.* https://www.simplypsychology.org/cognitive-dissonance.html

Mohan, S. (2021). *USER PERCEPTION TOWARDS OTT PLATFORMS (KERALA THRISSUR) User Perception Towards OTT Video Streaming Platforms in Kerala (With Special Reference to Thrissur). September.*

Mohanty, D. (2021). *There are more roles for females than males in OTT platforms. Is it true? We find out.* https://www.news9live.com/entertainment/there-are-more-roles-for-females-than-males-in-ott-platforms-is-it-true-we-find-out-24472.html?infinitescroll=1

Mukherjee, S. (2020). *Female's the way on OTT: Women-fronted stories rule the web | Bollywood - Hindustan Times.* https://www.hindustantimes.com/bollywood/female-s-the-way-on-ott-women-fronted-stories-rule-the-web/story-LAKPLLs95YGRt4wtXga3ZL.html

Outlook, P. (PWC) M. and E. (2020). *COVID19 spurs significant growth in India's OTT Consumption - IndBiz | Economic Diplomacy Division | IndBiz | Economic Diplomacy Division.* PriceWaterhouseCoopers (PWC) Media and Entertainment Outlook 2020. https://indbiz.gov.in/speedy-rise-in-ott-market-covids-boon-to-india/

Ravali, T. (2020). *Role of OTT Platforms.* https://www.stumagz.com/role-of-ott-platforms/

Sudhagoni, V. S., Adepu, N., & Teja Bellamkonda, S. (2020). *European Journal of Molecular & Clinical Medicine PROFILES AND PREFERENCES OF OTT USERS IN INDIAN PERSPECTIVE. 7*(8), 5106–5142.

Tapjoy. (2020). *What Is OTT? - Understanding The Modern Media Streaming Landscape - Tapjoy.* https://www.tapjoy.com/resources/what-is-ott/

Urgelles, A. (2017). The Threat of OTT for the Pay-TV Market. *Current and Emerging Issues in the Audiovisual Industry*, 19–38. https://doi.org/10.1002/9781119384632.CH2

"SEXUAL OBJECTIFICATION OF WOMEN IN TAMIL FILMS: PROVOKING REALITY" Epciba Immanuvel

Introduction:

"The film can be seen as a medium by which an individual realizes himself, his social function, and the values of his community (Fearing, 1947)."

Films are a very important element in our day-to-day life. Actors are regarded as role models by the common people. Actors set the trends and people tend to follow it without a blink of an eye, as it is here I would like to quote the motto of one of the popular Tamil Television Channels, **"Cinema is mixed in our blood"**. As cinema is close to our heart, close to our life, people tend to learn from it and they are exposed to certain content of the films an innumerable of time, they follow it without giving much thought. Tamil directors use female actors as attracting material, the thighs and hips of women are used as seducing material to catch the interest of the male audience and so they will spend their money to watch the film. Here is my question: Do the male audience learn from the films to treat women as sexual object in the reality?

Films have the power to influence the reality from provoking for freedom from dictatorship to persuade violence among humans. The purpose of this paper is to evince that sexually objectifying content of women in Tamil films provokes the reality that it makes men to sexually objectify the women in the real life. This study is conducted among the males of Tamil Nadu and Pondicherry. The paper is blended study of Critical approach and Post positivist approach. A structured questionnaire was designed for the purpose of data collection and total of 298 Tamil males responded for this survey through Google forms.

Review of Literature:

The first content, I took for Review of Literature was a Romanian Documentary named "Chuck Norris Vs Communism", directed by IlincaCălugăreanu released in the year 2015.*(Călugăreanu,2015)*.The documentary is about true incident how people overcame the 20 years of dictatorship of Nicole, by watching foreign films. Media were not allowed to telecast any programs but only the propaganda of the dictator, People started to smuggle foreign films and watch it at night. The foreign films taught them the knowledge of the free world and how people can be happy in the free world. This thirst for the freedom, led to the revolution and the dictatorship came to an end.

Another, content named "ReelumRealum, a Tamil Book written by Doctor Narayana Reddy. It consists of questions and answer that got published in a weekly magazine named "CiniKoothu", which then later complied in to this book "ReelumRealum, which means "Fake and Truth". I would like to highlight one of the questions asked by a person named K.P.Balakrishnan from Chennai. He said, "He wants to live a life like portrayed in the Tamil Film named "KeezhakuSimaiyile", in which actor would go to house of his mistress, have chicken food, take oil bath; which was followed by bedroom scenes(Reddy, 2002,p.10)". Another person, L.Ramanathan said that "he was provoked by rape scenes, even though he wants to oppose social defects (Reddy, 2002, p.88)".

Films influenced the notion of free world to Romanian People and so the dictatorship ended. People wish to be living the life like the way film portrays and see the women as sexual object in real life. These reviews of literature added strength to my notion: "FILM INFLUENCES REALITY"

Rationale and Objectives of the Study:

Nearly 200 films were released in the year 2019 in Tamil Nadu and think of the number of films released in Tamil, since its first sound film "Kalidas". Consider thinking about the position of females in these films. Majority of heroines serve as a material for male gaze. Over these years don't they create any impact on the audience?

According to the survey conducted by **Broadcast Audience Research Council of India** from November 2018 to October 2019, an individual consumes 293 hours which is 12 days in a year to watch films which are broadcasted only in television. When it is calculated for total life time, an individual spends approximately 2 years in his/her life time to watch films broadcasted only in television. The average life expectancy of Indians is 68.7 years in which 22.9 years (1/3rd) of life time is spend for sleeping. Out of the remaining years, 2 years spending only for watching films in television is a big deal. When we think of the time spend in theatres, OTT and scrolling across social media, how much time we would be spent in our life time to watch films or come across contents of films? So, there is high chance of being influenced by film.

It has already been established by a number of researchers that women are sexually objectified or sexualized in films; but, what are the impacts or repercussions in reality?

So, the statement of the problem of my research is to study the sexually objectifying women in Tamil films provoking men in reality and so the same is my objective and others are to study films are promoting sexual violence against women in reality; to study men's thinking about sexually objectification of women in the films; to study women empowering films uplift the status of women in the society.

Theoretical Framework:

In research from Mulvey, L. (1975), driven by the theories of Sigmund Freud and JacquesLacan, the author altered the orientation of cinema theory towards a psychoanalytic framework that presents classic Hollywood films as expressions of patriarchal ideology, in which the audience may identify with one of the characters (for example, a male actor) and experience the situations via that character. To them, women were shown as objects to be satisfied by a man, as enticing and beneath the male.

Ahmed and Wahab (2016) recite Mulvey'sthree types of male gaze that women in the movies are perceived with. They bring forth the fact that women are sexually objectified first and foremost by the **"male gaze"**from the eyes of the **Male Lead**, the **Camera**, and the **Male Audience** who tend to subject themselves in the place of the male protagonistof the film, and enjoy gazing at the female character as nothing but a mereentity for their sexual desires (Ahamed and Wahab, 2016).

As we see about Tamil audience here, we praise actors more and we are ready to make them as State leader by only seeing their characters and patriotism in films and by doing so, how much respect do the Tamil people hold for the actors?. So, male audiences identify them with the male protagonists in the films. This identification with male protagonists can lead to expect the woman as like female protagonists in the reality too like expectation of the beauty of women in physical rather than in her character and also immoral behaviours like catcalling and seeing women as sexual object and promoting violence against women in the reality.Everything in the film has made for male audience, then what about female audience; she has to experience the film secondarily by identification with male. Women have to watch women in the films from the point of view of a heterosexual male. I think, when women start to watch women in the films, in the position of heterosexual women, everything will seem wrong with the films.

Film not only teaches men to see women as sexual object, but also teaches women to objectify themselves in accordance with the wish of the men. Tamil film never teaches women to be independent and live on their own. It makes women to believe that they are always dependable on their father and husband. They are born to serve men and act as the way their men like and make men happy and look after children and be a good wife. The saddest thing is independent women are always shown as bad in Tamil films like Neelambari in Padaiyappa, Trisha in Kodi, Kajol in VIP 2, Reemasen in Vallavan, Sriya Reddy in thimuru.

Let me compare **Agenda settingtheory** of McCombe and Donald shaw (1976), that when a particular news is given more important than other news, then the audience will automatically perceive that particular news as the more important. The media sets the agenda to which have to be given more importance and according to it the audience react. Now let us think about the films from the earlier period to till now, most of the films have male gaze and portray women as sexual objects. The "Male gaze" in the agenda stands first among the Tamil films and don't they create any impact on the audience? The younger generation, who are still learning, won't they learn to objectify women?

According to **Reinforcement theory** of Klapper (1960), the violent depictions on television enhance whatever existing pattern of conduct among viewers when it comes to themedia-affecting-reality scenario. When this reinforcement theory is applied to the sexual objectification of women in movies, won't men who already have a patriarchal mind-set be reinforced even more and consider women as sexual objects?

Keeping Feminist theory of Laura Mulvey (1995), Agenda setting theory of McCombe and Donald Shaw (1976) and Reinforcement theory of

Klapper (1960) as guide, this study has been made.

Methodology:

A quantitative methodology of circulating a structured questionnaire is adopted for this study. Questionnaire is a reliable and rapid way of collecting data from a large number of samples in a timely and effective manner. Hence, it is the tool used for data collection. First, I framed a model questionnaire and asked out my male friends to answer the questionnaire. I seek out their opinion for improvisation of the questionnaire. Because, it is quiet difficult to bring out the true feeling especially in the cases like sexuality and its feeling. So, it takes me quite some days to work on it in order to make a questionnaire which is quite interesting and also to bring true answers out of men. The questionnaire consisted of 15 closed-ended questions with different likert scale but mainly two point likertscale.

As this study was upon men, the respondents are men only. It is totally on whether men provoked by the continuous exposure of sexually objectifying women content in the Tamil films. The male respondents are from Tamil Nadu and Pondicherry because the study is about Tamil males. The data has been collected through Google forms. I aimed for more than 100 respondents and the sampling method is purposive sampling, as the survey took place through Google forms. On 9th of April, 2020 I have started distributing my questionnaire through Google forms with the help of social media. On 8th of May, 2020 I have stopped accepting the responses. Within the period of one month, I receive 304 responses from around the different parts of Tamil Nadu and Pondicherry. Out of 304 responses, 6 responses are not answered fully and so the numbers of samplings are 298 only. The data thus collected are entered in Microsoft Excel and then analyzed and presented using simple percentages.

Frequent Films:

Throughout the rest of the article, I am going to talk about the majority of percentages because we rely on the majority for corroboration.

Data shows that the males between the age group 23-30 outnumbered the age group of other male respondents. 98 respondents are from the age group of 16 to 23; 149 respondents are from 23 to 30; 31 respondents from 31 to 40 and above 40 years of age is 20.

From the analysis, it is known **51.43%** of male respondents watch films **daily, 24.50%** of them watch **more thanthree films per week, 6.38%** watch **more thanthrice within two weeks** and **17.79%** watch **more thanthrice per month**. It is difficult to calculate how much films an individual watch within a period of time. But through this analysis, we came to know that half of the male respondents watch films daily.

Earlier, I have said that films take part in our day-to- day life. From the study, it is clear that half of the male respondents watch films daily. In which 68 male respondents from the age group of 23-30 say that they watch films daily, which is the highest among all other age groups. Films are one among the daily activities. We can agree with the fact that only small percentage of people read books now-a-days, but films, almost everyone watches it. Now, we can understand how much responsibility the films have to teach or deliver a good message. Especially in Tamil film industry, most of the films are commercial and its main theme is the macho hero and the sexually objectified heroine by the macho hero. Is this all taught by the films, which is one among the daily activities? And also remember that 2 years has been spending in an active lifetime to watch films telecasted in television alone! So, we have been exposed to incalculable number of times of films.

Age wise distribution: percentage of time of watching films

Age / Options	Daily	More than thrice per week	More than thrice within two weeks	More than thrice per month
16-22	47	16	9	26
23-30	68	44	10	27
31-40	22	9	0	0
Above 40	16	4	0	0
Total	153 (51.34%)	73 (24.50%)	19 (6.38%)	53 (17.79%)

Enter Caption

Influence:

81.88% of male respondents think that films influence reality and 94.97% of male respondents agree that films emote their feelings like happiness, sad and arousal.

75. 84% is not welcoming female actress appearing in body revealing costumes in Tamil films, but 74.5% of male respondents encounter scenes frequently and often in Tamil Films where female actresses appear sexy in terms of looks and costumes and 77.85% are thinking that females are used as sexual object in Tamil Films. Comparing these data, majority of the males are aware that female actors are used as sexual object that they encounter scenes a lot of times that females appear glamorously, yet they are emoted by the films. So, it is not in the audience's hand to be controlled or influenced by the films. Everyone can choose their own clothing that is their freedom but remember the most of the Tamil directors are male and they choose the female actress to appear sexy, that they are objectified sexually with the male gaze of male lead, camera and male audience as Mulvey,L (1975) described.

Beauty standard Vs Good heart:

88.93% of male respondents think that all the Tamil films don't have a need to sexy appearance of female and we can here accept that females are just used as seducing material for the male audience and they are successful in it.

70.81% of male respondents say that films make them attracted towards a beautifully appearing women rather than a good hearted woman. We can see in the films that heroine will be very white skinned girl and glamour, who is overrated and her friend will be fair or black skinned with usual or less than usual appearance, who is underrated. Films never make anything at the correct rate or don't portray anything as such as it is. This makes the heroine sexually objectified and side character woman objectified. Films except few never treat women in a good manner. Films should change the standardization of portraying the beauty of women, since it influences the reality like the way, Laura Mulvey said about the three ways woman can be looked at.

Analysing the data, it has been shown that the highest number of males from the age group of 22 to 30 said that they are attracted towards beautifully appearing women. Indian society believes 22 to 30 is the right age for getting married and these young adults see features of women rather than heart and fantasize universal beauty to be their wife and these pressures by the marriage mart lead women to low self-esteem, which in turn make them fall prey for cosmetic markets. Even though some women never drop their ears to all these pressures, please never underestimate the power of ambitious moms and aunts of Indian Society.

Age wise distribution of percentage of Men agreeing that films make them attracted towards a beautifully appearing woman

Age / Options	Yes	No
16-22	67	31
23-30	95	54
31-40	29	2
Above 40	20	0
Total	211(70.81%)	87(29.19%)

Enter Caption

Violence:

94.97% of male respondents agree that films emote their feelings and so, it is a follow-up question to check the reliability of the questionnaire and research and I asked the question one more time in a straight forward manner and 76.51% of male respondents get excited when female actresses appear more glamorously. Hence, the majority of the male respondents agree with both notions that films make them emoted and excited when females are used as attractive material.

64.09% of male respondents agree that films promote sexual violence against women in the society and 26.51% say that films may promote it. Let me give an example, the word 'Figure'. The fame of objectifying women as figure all goes to the films. We can hear school and college boys describe the women as "good and bad figure" by equating the body parts of her to perfectness. Groping, catcalling, stalking has been taught by the films and these are creating sexual violence against women in the real life. Even to saddest, stalking has been glorified as love by the Tamil Films like Remo. Given it the deep thought, we can understand that hero in disguise as nurse has been stalking the heroine and that is considered as romantic gesture.

Sexual Object:

60.07% of male respondents are influenced by the films, in which hero's having more than one relationship simultaneously. By seeing those kinds of contents, the films make them to have long for more than one relationship simultaneously in the reality. People may ask that it is not a big deal that adultery is now legalized, but we are living in the society that values morality and I reckon that values are only for women and will you accept it if a woman does it? Won't the society speak ill of her? If behaviour is wrong, it should be wrong for both the genders.

There are young generations who are still learning what is good and bad. What will happen if they see such kinds of films and learn from it that women are something like sexual object, purely are the entice of male pleasures. At the time of reading this article, we don't know how many children are watching movies that explicitly describe women as objects.

Time for Change:

78.19 % of male respondents say that films are degrading the image of women as sexual object in the society and 63.09% say that films teach or trigger them to think women as sexual object in the reality too. It is not in the spectator's control in learning those behaviours from the films, especially when offensive activities are politely disguised as romantic gestures. They are well aware of the women objectification but they can't stop them from being influenced by the films, because it is a powerful media.

The Gen Alpha is cleverer than any generations before because of the development of technology and its easy availability. The Gen Alpha mostly is school students, who already are well aware of every aspects of life. Thanks to technology and special thanks to Internet. I don't criticize the development of technology but its lack of boundary and power to infiltrate our life.

So, they can learn easily from the films along with other contents that obtainable at finger tips.

Age wise distribution of percentage of men agreeing that films teach them to think women as sexual object

Age / Options	Yes	No
16-22	50	48
23-30	89	60
31-40	29	2
Above 40	20	0
Total	188(63.09%)	110(36.91%)

Enter Caption

78.25% of male respondents want strict censorship in Tamil films. It is quite glad that majority of the male respondents want it, through this we can understand that they are trying not to think or treat women as sexual object. They are expecting Tamil Industry to change.

We are now come across the much corroboration that films are teaching men to treat women as either object or sexual object in the reality and films affect male audience without their knowledge. Every injustice against women has been normalized in the reality, which further films are reinforcing that normalization in the era of 21st century, where film contents are available in abundant of networks that we are encountering it every day, every minute in our life. After every struggles of women in the past, when equality is expected to dawn in the women's life, when younger generations are expected to respect women more than their previous generations, the main question strikes in the mind: Do the society moving towards greater good of women or it simply making the women again fall even more in the submissive pit?

90.06% of male respondents think that the women empowering films can uplift the status of women in the society.

Not only bad things, films can teach good things also and they can play a major role in empowering women by delivering powerful content to all genders. They can teach male how to respect women and their choices. It is the high time; the more women empowering films must be produced. Films must sow the seed of change and the society can reap the welfare of women.

REFERENCE

Adina (producer).Călugăreanu(director) .2015.*Chucknorris vs communism* (motion picture).Romania:Vernon film production

Ahmed, S., Wahab, A.J. (2016).*Entertainment to exploitation: A psycho-analysis of sexual objectification of women in films/cinema.*

Biber, S.N.H., Leavy, P.L., (2007) *Feminist research practice*

Mulvey, L. (1975). *Visual pleasure and narrative cinema*

Nair, B., Jain, J., &Rai, S.(2009). *Films and feminism: Female bodies and the male gaze: Laura Mulvey and Hindi Cinema.ss*

Reddy, N. (2002).*Reelum realum.*10,88

MEDIA REPRESENTATION OF THIRD GENDER: A STUDY OF SELECT HINDI WAVE SERIES David Lalhmachhuana and Dr. Sayan Dey

Introduction

The increased use of the internet and telecommunication devices has altered media consumers' institutional thinking. The growing desire of consumers to place a greater focus on tailored content has given rise to new platforms such as Over the Top (OTT). Digital narratives are leveling the gender playing field by addressing issues and storylines that are rarely seen on the big screen. Since the postmodern era, gender identity has been in constant motion. Gender identity, subjectivity, and representation have all been challenged by postcolonial theorists, feminists, and poststructuralists from various perspectives. As a result, the terms gender and sex have been at odds for a long time, resulting in new perceptions now and then. Third-gendered persons have long been an outcast in our culture, with little identification and portrayal in the mainstream media. It all began with the colonization of India by the British. When the British gained complete control of India and established the British East India Company, authorities attempted to impose western ideas and concepts on Indians. The Indian

Penal Code (Section 377) was created as a result of this where homosexuality was made illegal. Even though the Indian Penal Code (Section 377) was deemed unlawful on 6th September 2018, "Hijras" are still considered a societal outcast.

Cinema is a social mirror. It has proven to be a source of amusement, study, and escape due to its ability to transcend physical place and time. Bollywood, often known as Hindi cinema, continues to be the world's largest film producer and has a sizable audience of moviegoers. The most extensively distributed film in India is mainstream Hindi cinema. Many films and songs featuring transvestism of male characters depicting hijras, such as Rishi Kapoor in the movie RafooChakkar (1975)(Mushtaq& Ahmed, 2019) and Amitabh Bachchan as a eunuch in the movieLaawaris (1981)(Mushtaq& Ahmed, 2019), have a long history in Indian cinema. Love triangles were incorporated in the scripts of films like Andaz (1949) and Sangam (1964), but the essential story was about the friendship between the two male lead characters; the presence of a female character in such films was only to minimize the homosexual angle. (Mushtaq& Ahmed, 2019).In the late 1980s, Bollywood made its debut with a film on transgender individuals. Gay sidekicks continued to appear as humorous characters in films such as Hum HainRahiPyaarKe (1993), Raja Hindustani (1996), and Taal (1999) after the 1990s. Then came films like Bombay Boys (1998) and Split Wide Open (1999), which featured nuanced and serious LGBT characters. Sadak (1991), Bombay (1995), Tamanna (1997), Darmiyaan (1997), ShabnumMausi (2005), and Murder 2 (2011) were sensitive and tense films that featured hijras prominently(Mushtaq& Ahmed, 2019). The portrayal of sexual minorities in film and television has been tainted by social stereotypes, religious condemnation, and the very real fear of social stigma. The films that portray the third gender are commonly divided into two categories: art films that take the issues of the third gender seriously but are rarely directed at the Indian audience, and popular films that use it solely as a source of entertainment. While most Hindi films still rely on insulting and stereotyped portrayals of non-binary gender identities, regional films, particularly in South India, have witnessed some applause-worthy Trans representation in the last decade.

Over The top platforms are referred to as OTT platforms. OTT platforms have become increasingly popular in recent years, owing to people's different tastes and preferences. The days when people relied on television to broadcast their favorite shows are long gone. People nowadays use OTT services to watch movies and TV shows. Users choose their favourite genre and begin watching the content of their choice. Streaming platforms are supporting films and programs that would otherwise struggle to find producers and distributors.

One notable development following the COVID-19 epidemic and subsequent lockdowns was the increased consumption of content via over-the-top (OTT) platforms. With theatres closing, the epidemic forced the media and entertainment industries to adapt in ways they had never done before. OTT (Over the Top) platforms, is rapidly emerging in India. OTT content is not only structurally distinct from Bollywood theatrical releases, but it has also played a key role in portraying a new, multi-layered view of gendered identities in India.OTT ('Over the Top') platforms allow producers and authors to tell uncensored stories and films. Because these platforms are now uncensored, content broadcast on them has more artistic freedom. As a result, LGBTQ+ representation is becoming more visible. The audience has the opportunity to see and hear stories that are truly imaginative, unique, and diverse in origin and practice.While there has been a continuous progression in how the third gender is perceived and depicted on television over the last few decades, the movement has been too slow and steady to cause any genuine change in the broader narrative, which is still dominated by old dominating notions. However, with the rise of OTT and streaming platforms in recent years, both producers and spectators have been able to notice a different and more dramatic shift in the kind of third gender characters we see onscreen.'Made in Heaven' (Amazon Prime), 'Four More Shots' (Amazon Prime), 'Feels Like Ishq' (Netflix), 'AjeebDaastaans' (Netflix), and 'Call My Agent' (Netflix), among others, have homosexual protagonists in an Indian context. The third gender depiction in the Bollywood web series has been criticized for many years for its stereotypes.

Review of Literature

Mushtaq& Ahmed (2019) discover the identity creation of the third gender by examining Sadak. The article looks at the film's cinematography, sound, characters, dialogues, mise-en-scene, etc. It concludes that the film presents transgender people as villains, sending a negative message about the third gender to the viewer.

Afshana& Din (2017),examines several ground-breaking films that have succeeded in presenting highly realistic third gender features, attempting to break out from the customary limits of portraying the stereotypical third gender on film.A study was done on selected Bollywood movies, 1. Sadak(1991), 2. Tamanna(1997), 3.Shabnum Mausi (2005) and 4. Welcome to Sajanpur (2008) and concludes that all of the films moved away from the usual portrayal of Hijras as fillers or in comedy settings with no real characterization, and instead challenged stereotypical views about the third gender in India, depicting them in a humanistic way and occasionally with shades of grey.

Bhattacharjee (2014) tries to highlight the depiction of the third gender in the Bollywood film 'Chitrangada'. It concludes that Indian films about the third gender follow the same pattern as other films about the third gender around the world. Chitrangada focuses on the many facets of the challenge that a member of the third gender community faces starting with the question of the matter's acceptability or non-acceptability among family members, to the technical hurdle of a child's adaptation, to the marriage of two gay men without a legitimate mainstream sex code, everything is examined in detail.

Sharma (2021) examines how the structure of the Indian web series affects gender representation and hate speech on modern and digital platforms. The article concludes that hate speech is frequently used in web series and online streaming entertainment in terms of abusive language and gender discrimination and that all of this has a significant impact on society. It also concludes that in India, the web series culture has brought about many changes in our society, as well as personal effects on individuals.

Shah (2021) analyses the influence of queer representation on OTT services on audiences. AjeebDastaans, PaavaKadhaigal are the movies being analysed. It concludes that these films have had a good impact on Indian society's perceptions. It is raising awareness and assisting in the normalization of LGBT identities. It encourages people to explore their sexuality and accept it as normal rather than a sin.

Objectives

- To analyze how the third gender is portrayed in selected Hindi wave series.
- To analyze how third gender representation has evolved so far in the Hindi wave series.

Research Method

The study is qualitative and employs a textual analysis method. Here, certain characters from a selected Hindi wave series will be analyzed to find out how they are portrayed in the web series.

Sample Studied

1. **PatiPatniAurPanga (2020)**
2. **Sacred Games (2018)**
3. **Paurashpur (2020)**

1.PatiPatniAurPanga (2020): Directed by AbirSengupta, it is a Hindi web series which was released on December 11, 2020, staring Adah Sharma, Naveen Katsuria, HitenTejwani, GurpreetSaini, and Alka Amin. The web series falls under the comedy-drama genre and contains 6 episodes. The story revolves around Romanchak who is a sub-broker and Shivaniwho was looking for a place to stay in Mumbai. After touring several homes, they discover that none of the owners are interested in renting to a bachelor woman. Romanchak persuaded his parents to set aside one room in his home for a PG, and he managed to convince Shivani to stay in his home as a PG.Shivani became friendly with Romanchak's family and they admired her greatly. And it didn't take long for the acquaintance to turn into friendship, friendship to turn into a love affair, a love affair to marriage. After a few days after their marriage, Romanchak started to doubt Shivani as she has no friends, no family, and no records about her past. Romanchak started digging deeper and deeper and found out that his wife Shivani have gone through a sex reassignment surgery and became a woman. After finding out the truth about Shivani, he wanted to get a divorce but Shivani did not want to sign the divorce paper and also refuse to leave the house. Romanchak and his mother went to a lawyer who assures them that there is no chance that Shivani can win the case. While Shivani was looking for a lawyer, she was either discouraged or either reject her case by other lawyers and in the end, she represent herself in court. Shivani decided to sign the divorce paper and their part their ways. In the end, Romanchak finally realized his mistakes and he decided to go back to her.

2. Sacred Games (2018): Directed by AnuragKashyap and VikramadityaMotwane, it is a Hindi web series released on 5 July 2018 (Season 1) and 15 August 2019 (Season 2) starring Saif Ali Khan, NawazuddinSiddiqui, RadhikaApte, PankajTripathi, KalkiKoechlin, RanvirShorey. It was the first Indian Netflix original series and contains

16 episodes. The story revolves around Satraj, a policeman who got a call from Ganesh Gaitonde, a crime overlord who instructs Satraj to liberate Mumbai in 25 days, setting off a chain of events that reaches deep into India's underground. Sartaj tracks Gaintonde's phone calls and sees the gangster shoot himself in the head when he was about to be apprehended. The 25-day countdown to Mumbai's destruction begins with Gaitonde's death. The audience is introduced to Gaitonde's flashback where his past life and actions led him to become a crime lord. After Satraj was suspended, he works with Anjali Mathur a Research and Analysis Wing (RAW) agent tasked with solving this case. In the end, the cops learn of Malcolm's role in Anjali's murder, and Trivedi is discovered in Gaitonde's underground hideout.

3. Paurashpur (2020): Directed by Sachindra Vats, it is a Hindi web series which was released on December 25, 2020, staring AnnuKapoor, MilindSoman, ShilpaShinde, Shaheer Sheikh, Flora Saini, AdityaLal, Anat Joshi, SahilSalathia, Poulomi Das, KashishRai, AshmitaBakshi. The web series falls under Historical Drama and contains 7 episodes. It is a story about a mythical place called 'Paurashpur' that is ruled by King BhadraPratap Singh in the 16th century. A patriarchal society is depicted by the fact that the entire kingdom is ruled by male ideas. BhadraPratap Singh, the land's monarch, is a comparatively old man whose mind is constantly flooded with his sexual desires. He marries young queens to fulfill his desires. His ideals are having a devastating effect on the entire realm. Women have little value in Paurashpur and they are merely exploited by society's men. Women are also required to follow the centuries-old ritual of sati and to wear chastity belts. The story revolves around the missing queens who were kidnapped by the mysterious kidnapper "Nakaabposh" and how women and the third gender fight for equality.

Discussion

PatiPatniAurPanga (2020): The web series tries to tackle what the third gender people are facing in real life, but still portrayed the third gender as a societal outcast. The portrayal of the third gender in this web series is almost the same as the earlier Bollywood movies where third genders are used as a source for comedic purposes. In the story, we still see people are transphobic about the third gender. We can say that the story did not do justice to the third-gender community. They still portrayed them as societal outcasts and used them as comic reliefs.

Sacred Games (2018): The web series uniquely portrayed the third gender. We can see the representation of the Third gender character called " Kukoo". Kukoo was portrayed as a strong, intelligent, and independent woman who brings good luck. The way the web series portrayed her was different from previous Bollywood movies. Instead of seeing her as a disgrace in society, everybody sought after her. She was portrayed as a strong character that carried herself and commanded men around her. The stereotypic portrayal of the Third Gender is absent in Sacred Games.

Paurashpur(2020): The web series portrayed the third gender as no other Indian visual has portrayed before. This web series uses a Third Gender character "Boris" as a protagonist who plays a huge role in moving the stories forward. Boris was shown as a fighter who fought against injustice in the kingdom. The web series portray the advantages of being a third gender as they are exempted from the rules of Paurashpur as the rules only apply to men and women. Taking in context of the character Boris, he was strong, intelligent, and fight against injustice same as most Bollywood heroes.

From the sample studied, we can see that both Sacred Games and Paurashpur have a unique take on the third gender. They move away from the stereotypical portrayal of third-gender characters which we used to see in early Bollywood movies. Third gender characters from these two web series (Boris and Kukoo) are represented as strong, intelligent characters whereas, in PatiPatniAurPanga, third gender characters are still represented as comic relief or are used to elicit humor which is present in most Bollywood movies. PatiPatniAurPanga attempts to push third gender identification, concerns, and relationships from the margins of mainstream Bollywood to the foreground by challenging stereotypical views about the third gender in India, depicting them in a humanistic way at the end of the series but the negative portrayal of the third gender outweighs the positive portrayal. Bollywood movies usually represent the third gender as a villain, where the Indian audience's minds are swayed towards this concept of the third gender as a villain however in Paurashpur, it changes this concept by having the third gender as a protagonist. This type of web series is new to the audience. The role of Boris in Paurashpur came as a revolution in the portrayal of the third gender, as in the web series, the third gender was brought into the center from the beginning. The web series not only breaks the mold by bringing the third gender to the center but also shattered the norm of a masculine hero in Hindi cinema by casting the third gender as a hero. The depiction of the third gender as a brave and skilled fighter is a way of vindication from the age-old satirical portrayal of the third gender. Similarly in the web series Sacred Games, the web series brings the third gender character as an independent character that every man wanted for her charm. The web series breaks away from the satirical portrayal of the third gender as disgusting and scary with the character "Kukoo" as an attractive character.

Conclusions

The western mindset of despising and marginalizing anyone who was not straight or androgynous gained hold in Indian society. The Hijra community was forced to transform from revered religious and governmental figures to social outcasts. As a result of their social exile, Hijras face economic and physical difficulties. Hijras are more prone to have financial troubles as a result of the stigma they face. They are denied educational opportunities, career opportunities, and prejudice in every aspect of their lives(indug, 2018). Because of the domination of heterosexuality over non-heterosexuality over the years, the dichotomous gender and the third gender have been depicted in our society in a typical colonial way to make them culturally real. The binary gender's status is regarded as natural and desirable, whereas gender variants' status is regarded as unnatural and outcast. The presence of tales like these serves as the foundation for one sex's supremacy over the other. The dominant sex writes and rewrites the third gender's body from time to time, resulting in them losing control over their bodies and identities(Yates, 2014),. Throughout this process, the third gender is marginalized and, as a result, stereotyped by the filmmakers. Accordingly, the media's portrayal of transgender characters for the most part is unethical. Trans-people are used to make stories more exciting and to boost attention so that the producers may make more money. Stereotypes are used and accepted as genuine human judgments, while the transgender community's struggles are minimized and used as comic relief. These ideas are then reinforced in the minds of viewers who have no prior knowledge of transgender identity. The media will not provide more responsible and honest portrayals of transgender characters until the audience demands it.

The three web series PatiPatniAurPanga (2020), Sacred Games (2018), and Paurashpur(2020) bring the character of the third gender into a serious and open space. While analyzing the web series, the third gender characters are responsible for moving the entire story which is rarely seen in Indian visual medium. PatiPatniAurPanga (2020) shows how the Indian community views the third gender and still used the stereotypical portrayal of the third gender in the series but tries to rectify the problems faced by them in an emotional way. Sacred Games (2018) brings life to the third gender character called "Kukoo". She was portrayed as a beautiful dancer, and every man falls for her, which is hardly seen in Bollywood movies. The good luck or magic that the Hijra brings is also portrayed in this web series which is neglected or forgotten by most Indian audiences. A strong, independent trans character whom everyone wanted is hardly present in Bollywood movies and Sacred Games has managed to shine a light on this aspect. Paurashpur(2020) uses a third gender character as the main protagonist. He was shown to be a strong, great fighter who fought for inequality. This type of story is new to Indian audiences as third genders are usually shown to be weak or their roles are minor. The web series reverse the view of third gender characters in Paurashpur which was used to be seen in Bollywood movies, especially in the 90s.

With the help of the sample studied, we can conclude that the representation of the third gender in the Hindi waves series has changed dramatically in terms of characters and the role that they play.

Limitations of the study

The study was restricted to how the third gender is portrayed in selected Hindi waves series and did not take into account the in-depth narrative of the web series. Secondly, the study was done only on selected Hindi web series where some of the characters have a limited screen time and a web series can always be renewed with new seasons, and the introduction of new characters is possible.

Suggestions for further research

Given the scarcity of significant research on the selected Hindi wave series, this study may pave the way for future research in this field. Future research can build on the findings of this study to derive key conclusions and go into previously unexplored elements of the subject.

A study on the representation of females in selected Hindi waves series could also give a different perspective to this research and can be used as a documented source for future reference.

References

Afshana, S., & Din, H. (2017). Portraying Third Gender: A Study of Select Bollywood Movies. *International Journal of Interdisciplinary and*

Multidisciplinary Studies, 4(3), 60–68.

Banu, Ap., Professor, A., & Yasmin, D. (2020). History of Transgender Portrayal in Indian Cinema. *International Journal of Research and Analytical Reviews (IJRAR) Www.Ijrar.Org*, 7(1), 206. www.ijrar.org

Bhattacharjee, J. (2014). Third Gender in Indian Films with a special Reflection on Chitrangada. *International Journal of Scientific and Research Publications*, 4(1), 2250–3153. www.ijsrp.org

indug, A. (2018, October 29). *India's relationship with the third gender*. UAB Institute for Human Rights Blog. Retrieved May 23, 2022, from https://sites.uab.edu/humanrights/2018/10/29/indias-relationship-with-the-third-gender/

Mushtaq, T., & Ahmed, D. A. (2019). Third Gender Portrayal in Bollywood: An Analysis of Sadak. *International Journal of Trend in Scientific Research and Development*, *Volume-3*(Issue-3), 17–22. https://doi.org/10.31142/ijtsrd21636

Ravi, R. (2020). *Transgender in India: A Semiotic and Reception Analysis of Bollywood Movies.*

Sharma, M. K. (2021). " *Emerging Gender Role and Hate Speech Representation in Indian web series OTT media Content .*"8(11), 158–173.

The third gender and hijras.(n.d.).Religion and Public Life at Harvard Divinity School.https://rpl.hds.harvard.edu/religion-context/case-studies/gender/third-gender-and-hijras

Web series. (2007, April 16). Wikipedia, the free encyclopedia. Retrieved March 9, 2022, from https://en.wikipedia.org/wiki/Web_series

Yates, S. (2014). Power-Knowledge. In *Encyclopedia of Critical Psychology*. https://doi.org/10.1007/978-1-4614-5583-7_438

ACKNOWLEDGE ME": REPRESENTATIONS OF TRANSGENDER IN INDIAN MEDIA AND THEIR REALITIES Dr.Shweta Chaudhary, Dr.Rakesh Kumar Yogi and Dr.Deepika

Introduction

In recent years, the transgender and gender diverse population has gained a stronger voice in the American media representation. Although these voices are being heard, there are limits on the types of transgender representation displayed in media (Mocarski et al. 2019: 416).Coinciding with rising number of media portrayals, there has been also an increase in stereotypical and negative portrayals that do not accurately reflect the real experiences of transgender people. Both in terms of qualitative as well as quantitative the transgender representation across all forms of media is an issue and has been overwhelmingly problematic(see Jobe 2013, Poole 2017, Reitz 2017,McLaren 2018 andMocarski et al. 2019)

In many Bollywood movies trans-people are represented as an object of entertainment for instance in movie *Maine PyarKiya* (1989), *PyarKiyaToDarnaKya* (1998) and *Dil Ne JiseApnaKaha* (2004) their personalities and mannerism are shown in funny and comic gestures. In movies such as *Sadak* (1991), *Sangharsh* (1999) and *ShabnamMausi* (2005) transgender people were showcased as criminal or villain (see Bhattacharjee 2014, Chaudhary2019, Mushtaq and Ahmed 2019). ParidhiChaudharyin her study "Stereotypical representation of marginalized transgender characters in Indian canon" claimed that "Hijrasare always shown as either very villainous or unrepresented character. No normal Hijra character has ever emerged to make a mark on public's mind" (Chaudhary 2019, 103).She claimed that the funny scene in representations wheretransgender people are mainly depicted attracted toward opposite gender specifically to a man and questioned that why all hijras in Bollywood movies are in love with men, no one knows. Further her study assumed and then found that these representations are probably used to make the audience laugh (Chaudhary2019, 103).

Since passing centuries there are no changes observed in media representations of transgenderIn, recent Bollywood movies such as *Laxmi* (2020) and *Gangubai* (2022) the transgender characters are shown as a symbol of violence and aggression.Bhattacharjeeclaimed in his study "Third Gender in Indian Films with a special Reflection on Chitrangada" thattheissue of third gender has not occupied much space in Indian media and filmic communication have very often showed the third gender recalling as a (*Chhakka or Hijra*)character, and if sometimes thenspecifically to add humour to the content.It is arguable in this context that media representation has not focused much with the third gender question, (such as the lack of acceptability in society, how they faced discrimination at public places, do they have access to good quality life, do they fit in the position of doctor, teacher, entrepreneur etc) as some research in India found that the media mis-represent third-gender identities and portray their appearance in unrealistic way that has no relations with their everyday life realities and struggles(Jain 2015, Afshana and Din 2017) these studies have also focussed on "lacks a basis in fieldwork or intensive interviewing"with transgender people (Afshana and Din 2017, 32).

"Media influence attitudes, behaviours, and shapes individuals' ideas of world[1] (Gerbner et al. 1985:18). Somewhat similar from the Gerbner's ideas, this paper examined the relationship between media representations of transgender people, and the ways in which sample respondents relate to them in realities. Do these representations play any role in framing their identities among society? It also finds out how poor and struggling respondents, watch their under-represented (or misrepresented) images in media, what they feel about such representations and in what ways they relate them with their ideas. It also aimed to find out people opinion for transgender communities (such as men and women perception on third gender realities and representations, in the ways they recall them, discuss them in their lives. Finally,it also detailed on the media habits of transgender community (such as accumulation and ownership patterns of media goods, programming choices, time spent on medium etc).

In recent decades, the liberalisation process accelerated the interaction of the Indian people with global forces of consumption and television became an important agent of those cultural influences that contributed directly to the acceleration of consumption patterns among Indian people. The role of advertising has been seen as critical in promoting the new ethos of consumerism (Johnson 2005:42-43). In similar context this paperexplores the ways in which watching representation/ advertisingrelated to or were helpful in providing new modern possibilities of lifestyles and life chances (such as change in clothing, hairstyle, mannerism etc) to transgender people. It looks particularly into cultural aspects of use of media and its influences on ideas, opportunities and life chances.

Objective and Questions

The paper aimed to know the perspectives of transgender people in various media representations. As media habits are the basis for any media analysis studies so therefor before proceeding for representational analyses, this paper also provides detailed account of respondent's everyday media habits. Watching representationsrelated to or were helpful in providing new modern possibilities of lifestyles and life chances to transgender people in realities; and negotiate with or adopt aspects of these symbolic works in developing their own styles (such as clothes, hairstyles and fashion).

It also attempted to discuss the experiences of transgender community on how and in what ways media can create sensitisation on the issues of their struggles and realities among other genders in society in the way people recall or remember them.

1. What kind of patterns of accumulation can be traced both in terms of media goods and habits? What programmes are watched and in what ways can their viewing patterns be stratified?

2. Do these representations relate with the experiences and everyday cultures of transgender people?
3. Do these characters have any relation with the lives of trans-people in realities?
4. Do these representations are responsible in identity framing or behaviour changes in society?
5. Are these engagements seen as useful or helpful in providing opportunities and intersect with life chances in any positive ways?

Theoretical framework

In previous long case study engagement withGurugram and Delhi transgender people (see Yogi et al. 2022), wefound out how poor and struggling respondents,shared understanding of their marginalization and lived experiences, in their own voicesinclude regrets such as, family, peer group and society calling them *'chhakaa'* and *'hijra'*. We also contribute their independent thinking and ideas on importantissues and perspectives for living (such as dressing, access to education, employment and entertainment) rather than influence moreover are reason for humour, but it does not influence. Within this context present paper is an attempt to find out how and in what ways such ideas and thinking are influenced by media. As in Gerbnerand colleagues had suggested in their work "Living with Television: The Dynamics of the Cultivation Process" that people's perceptions of the world don't necessarily match reality (Gerbner et al. 1985:17). These views were a reflection of the idea that people's perceptionof the world becomes reflective of what is communicated through media and as a result shapes the way people behave.

According to Gerbner ideas Media influence attitudes, behaviours, and shapes individual's ideas of world[2] (Gerbner et al. 1985:18). Somewhat similar from the Gerbner's ideas, this paper examined the relationship between media representations of transgender people, and the ways in which respondentsrelate to them; observing that transgender people believed that media represents these poor struggling respondents as significantly poorer, funny characters, violent and criminal than is really the case. Also, Cultivation theory (Gerbner 1960) is adopted and was useful in defining media habits of transgender people in differentiating their behaviours (such as time of consumption, type of consumption, use of medium etc).

Methodology

This paper findings are based on quantitative analysis method. It is based on a survey where data was collected with two separate respondents' group one group belongs to transgender people and second group of people including men and women of age between 20-40.They are further divided into class intervals i.e20-25, 25-30, 30-35 and35-40.The data was collected through anelectronic google form closed ended questionnaire, containing various attributes relating to the study and was shared with people through social media Facebook groups. However, we received 58 Responses but only 50 responses for men and women groups were used and 30 responses for transgender people.

In addition, purposive samples of20transgender respondents selected from age group of 20-60 further they are divided into class intervals i.e20-30, 30-40, 40-50 and 50-60. These samples size was useful to access, ownership, accumulation and stratification patterns in terms of access to media and use of commodities; and other factors like income, age, gender, education, religion. As Bruce L. Berg argued that the logic of using a sample of subjects is to make interpretations about some larger population from a smaller one the sample (1988:30). From the perspective of qualitative research, researcher is largely concerned with purposive or judgmental sampling and to developing a purposive sample; researchers use their special knowledge about the area and population or group. For instance, Berg claimed that purposive samples are selected after field investigations on population or group, in order to confirm that certain types of individuals or persons processing certain qualities are included as a sample (Berg 1988:32). Therefore, to develop sample a pilot study was conducted in Bindapur, Janakpuri Delhito get preliminary understanding of these samples and their media access, media reach, programming choices, watching habits and ownership patterns of media use.

Media Histories of Transgender's

Transgender People recall that they would spend their time in earlier years by gossiping or chatting with each other inside 'gharana'sometimes they also move to other gharanafor celebrations. Entertainment for them was a community-based exercise, that is now replaced through mediated communication and in the process, has become a more private[3]. During the visit at a Gharanait was noticed that sometimes guru and chela watched television together. Previously they would spend their evenings by chatting with each other, because there was little else to do beyond household and professional work. Many transgender respondents remembered that, they would gather in the living area sit together in the evenings, and chat, dance or gossip about their wardrobe shopping. For young transgender, life was very restricted in evenings as they were not supposed to go out after 6 o'clock.Munni says, "Now I still sit in living areas in evening but I can see that all those gossiping and sharing are disappearing. Everyone goes to their room. Everything has changed and everyone has a busy life. *'Jyadatarchele'* (most chela) are engaged in watching television or operating their mobiles".

The advent of television has ended the differences in language many residents believe that television content has reached many homes with new information's that breaks the barrier of the print media, as well as English language literacy. Munni added that at their gharana, first television set was a black and white CRT (cathode ray tube) BPL television set that is now replaced with an LCD (liquid crystal display) television with TATA sky connection. She bought it fiveyears ago to watch movies and to entertain her. Resident says after 2000 the advent of satellite television connections and cable television has accelerated the spread of television in their areas. Nowadays they are moving towards paying 'packages' because with these packages they get to watch private channels (such as Life OK, Colors, Star Plus, Zee tv, Zee cinemaetc), for some transgender respondents in Bindapur, these channels services are 'source' for learning fashion and language skills.

As they discussed, that media content has influenced their perceptions of changes in their language, standard of living, ideas about their gender issues. They can also dub or convert English programs into Hindi via Tata sky so now entertainment is possible in every situation. Some of them have Tata sky connections while some have cable connection. Some young respondent say language is not a barrier in watching English programs as they can dub the English programmes in Hindi and watch them.Older respondents recall days in years gone by when television was brought home for the purpose of entertainment or fun. Through during fieldwork, it was observed that television viewing was not merely an activity of entertainment for them but this technology had serving as a source, from where they learned and enhanced their knowledge on different matters and issues of day-to-day life. During field work many trans-respondents say that their lifestyle has gone through major changes in recent years, with much higher spending also on modern gadgets and services like smart phone, LCD television, WIFI connections, cableand dish television connections.

The first television set in their gharanawas owned by (Late) Kamlain 1996. It was an ordinary second hand black and white set. Shewas a second guru of their gharanaand after that Munni is itself taking the responsibility of gharana since 2000 onward after her death. Later on, the first colour television set to come to gharana was also purchased by Munni in 2004. However, she added that now almost every gharana situated in Bindapur, Uttam Nagar and Sagarpurhas a television set even LCD television;but the first LCD television too was purchased by her chela in2011 on easy instalment basis.

Clinard points out that the basic to the problem of urbanization and urbanism is the decline in effective intimate communication among the members of a society and the effect of this decline is on social control of behaviour (Clinard, 1967, p 56). He claimed that "community development is more functional and process-oriented" and the social change can only derive through self-help. Clinard claimed that in many studies it is observed that media is giving spaces to community development and motivating people for self-help through diverse narratives and programming that become gateways for providing information for new shifts in lifestyle and culture. Television gave people with the ideas and information of new possibilities and better lifestyle that made many of people to become self-reliant (Clinard, 1967, p. 133-134). In summary in Bindapurgharana it was found, that transgender people, have access to most lifestyle goods that the urban middle class have; perhaps one can only find the difference in the scale of which they receive it. Many respondents spoke of the importance of content of television, YouTube and social media now as number of television sets, mobile phone, use of medium is much higher in these gharana's and its influences are greater also. With the evolution of media content post liberalization, mediated communication among transgender people, is used for entertainment, but also for information and opportunities that have relationship to shifts in life chances and trajectories to some extent.

Media Goods and Habits

In the month of March and April a survey was conducted to study media viewing habits, ownership of access to media goods, much including television, radio, newspaper, mobile phones and internet etc) in Bindapur area. Therefore,this section, detailed these aspects of ownership and media practices. The survey included question on access to television sets, type of television sets owned/acquired, mobile set, amount paid for connection etc.

Media goods, and viewing practices are based on among transgender living in gharanain the year (2022) that was collected with the help of survey of 30 transgender samples.This data was collected using closed questionnaire.

The survey found that the availability of media goods like television, cable or satellite and other commodity goods diffusion has reached surprising percentage in among transgender people in gharana of Bindapur. For instance, respondents told that during last 10-15 years there is rapid growth in television access, mobile phone accessand many trans-people have televisions, cable television or even satellite television. During my fieldwork, I found that many trans-people has reached to television and smart phone; and watches the programming from the comfort of their tiny homes and generate meanings in similar context as people make in other urban and rural settings. But the difference between their watching patterns is that nothing that they see in these media contents/programs is a reflection of 'culture' of their own everyday lives. The information's televised by these programs represent their places, locations and life in a negative way that are infect they say are not quite different from their realities. There social world and life is represented in rare situations and it is always in negative way showing them as beggar, evil and sometime comic. These negative representations that are frequently coming from television may create the image of their world as feelings of inferiority, humorous and even anger.

Television, mobile and internet ownership are highest as compared to other mediums (such as radio and newspaper access) (see annexure-1 for details) almost every respondentsaidthey had a television set with access to cable and satellite connectivity. Some respondents have new set; some of them have second-hand set. Almostevery respondent hasLCD set andalso have access to cable television and access to DTH connections like Airtel, Videocon and Tata Sky; an average amount between 300Rs to 1000Rs was paid monthly for these connections to access their favourite programmes and content. Respondent said they had access to media at more times and in more ways than ever before in their living rooms and bedrooms.

Their media consumption and usage timings vary from viewer to viewer and are influenced by their everyday lifestyle. Some of them say that being 'working' they do not get enough time to use media mediums; however, still these respondents generally manage to use media medium for 2-3 hour daily. Some young respondents use these medium for 4-5 hours everyday. Old age transgender respondents who are particularly illiterate and leads the gharana as guru's said use these mediums specifically television for long hours (approximately for 8-12 hour per day) to spend their time. Televisionwatching along with the use of YouTube and Facebookwas found as the most prevalent form of media usage among respondent in Bindapur, but the way they access and use is different for each and also has changed. While they watch television, they say they often simultaneously do something else. Similar to Mankekar's observations that "most of the women half-watched, half-listened while cooking, serving food, doing dishes, or sweeping the floor, they were nonetheless able to engage intimately with what they 'viewed' (1993, p. 548); some respondents for instance said they do daily household work (like cutting vegetable, ironing cloth, folding cloth cooking etc) while watching television or using mobile phone simultaneously; and they get entertainment with work. Some gurus of gharana (age 60 and above) said they watch television to pass their day time as they do not have any work to do. There was no television when they were young; people of their age used to spend their time in singing Hindi songs and learning dance steps, even today they do not feel to watch television. Theother members (chelas) are busy in their routines and they do not have social circle to gossip thus television seemed to be a 'time pass' activity for them.

Many respondents say that the media representation/content is available diversely with new themes of contemporary social relevance however respondent encountered oppositional readings by saying these contents are bold, sensationalized, not worthy to watch as these are not related with their life in significant way. Dissimilar to PurnimaMankekar (1993, p. 548) findings that generally women control the remote and programming decisions in family's in many transgender people that are surveyed said they had equal opportunities to control the remote and to watch the programming of their own choices; some young respondent said they have an individual chance and choices to watch television as their daily lifestyle (such as, profession work condition, no of television sets, work time, number of rooms) gave them these open chances to watch television and to use other media platforms such as Facebook, Instagram, YouTube etc; however in some cases it was witnessed in that few respondents responses where the television remote control is far more in the hands of other member of gharana (guru or other chela), particularly in gharanawhich possess only a single television set.

Mostly transgender respondents prefer to watch movie channels (such as Zee Cinema, Star Gold and Setmax) some transgender prefer to watch channel (such as Life Ok, Star Plus and Colors) lightly followed by Zee TV and Sony Entertainment. Mostly young transgender respondents watch channels MTV and 9XM. Theolder generation age between (50-60) mostly watches Hindi Movies. They can easily afford the monthly cost of television connections, mobile dataand WIFI connections. As a greater number of chela's are working. It was found that Colors and Star Plus followed by Zee cinema were the 'regularly viewed' channels. Colors was the most frequently watched channel at one time of field work with its programme '*Shakti AstitvaekEhsaaski*'(daily Hindi Soap based on transgender character life) regularly watched by transgender people of all age.

Also, the crime programme *Saavdhan* India on channel Life OK seemed in particular to be a genre of programming that derives television viewing habits of most of my viewers, followed by religious epics *Mahabharat* on channel Star Plus followed by Reality shows *Big Boss, MTV Roadies* and *Splitsvilla* and Music shows on 9xm. Development programmes/advertising are less watched because of its uncertain on-air timing, but respondents did sometimes watch them. Viewers mainly preferred to watch Hindi language programmes, the regional language programmes were watched occasionally (such as Punjabi and Haryanvi) however some young transgender including single respondents (belong to Christianity) said they like watching English program.

While looking at the ownership, viewership patterns and its reach, it was found that television was followed closely by mobile phones. Many respondents were using smart phone while only few of them are using basic handsets of mobile, many respondents didn't know how to operate them properly but used mobiles to communicate with other members. Many young respondents were using smart phones for the purpose of Facebook, What's-app, for making videos, watching YouTube content, messaging, video calling and androids gaming etc. Some of them are using new handsets while others are using second handsets. Most transgender people are not brand conscious they want to buy bigger one whatever brand it may be (Lava, Micromax, Oneplus, Xiomi or Spice) however few of them have access to apple gadgets too. It was easy for them to buy these brands and they can access features to connect with mediums. It was also found that MI Xiomi smartphones are at greater number preference because they felt Xiomi was a "branded phone' with all latest features which they could afford within their budget. Mostly transgender respondents frequently prefer to watch cinema on television and occasionally watch movies in cinema halls, they generally pay 300-500 Rs for movie tickets and they can easily afford the cost of ticket. Many respondents said that yes,they have to face both social as well as physical discriminations at the time of their visit at cinema halls.

Itwas witnessed that mostly respondent uses more than one medium and have more than one content choice. There was no frequency of radio and newspaper reading was found. Television and you tube were preferred as heavily assessed mediums as respondents said, it's a lively medium; both listening and watching "go parallel", and that they said helped connect them with the medium in a way that is not possible in the case of radio. Print consumption is also absent due to high rate of illiteracy and those who are literate they say read text sometime available online at website. These viewing habits seem suggest that except television there is a possible reach and use of other medium of mediated communication among transgender community, however these possibilities or influences are depended on other factors such as education, income, age and other attributes (such as availability of resources and needs).

Relationship between transgender respondents and mediated representation

In many instances it was found that transgender respondents drew connections between television programming their decisions, choices, style and fashions, perceptions, attitudes, conversations (style and language), consumer choices (in terms of purchase of commodities) and life aspirations (in terms of marriage, educational goals, status, income and identity formationetc). It was observed that many respondentsuse diverse media medium;thus, access to diverse content and also relate to them both as preferred and oppositional readings as suggested by Hall (1980); however, factors such as age, education, religion, class, caste and income were often the prominent determinants, for their different engagements with programming that also not have any connections in making readings. Some young respondent say they have emotional relationships with specific television content (recalled Hindi Soap '*Shakti AstitvaekEhsaaski*' based on a story of transgender women who get married with a normal man and their struggling everyday life) because they believe that it gave them with some hopes of future possibilities. So, some respondent precept them as preferred reading and some respond them as oppositional reading.It reflects the social life of their society and their culture.Theseprogrammes sometime have connections with their own daily lives to some extent for instance they say in the way representation shown them in baby-shower blessings in some dancing clips but at the same time are not significantly useful in any ways as they are not giving any possibility of change infect this content, they say are more responsible in promoting their negative images in society. However, at the same time some television women characters provide them access to fashion trends. On other hand some literate/educated respondents have a noticeably more diverse (and individual) relationships with content; they were less dependent and less attached to mediated mediums and only access these to amuse themselves. However, they were alienated with political news and current affairs because news programming's have no spaces and voice for their positive developments. Many admit that their lives have changed in past decades. some transgender respondent also feels connected with mythological epic and religious programming. Some respondent also watches reality shows that they say enhance their learning process.

Structures of power and authority in member relations were visible in watching decisions; in holding of the remote, schedules of sitting around television sets, and in making program selections. Such hierarchy were seen in gharana that occupied single television set, and in circumstances of sitting together and watching programmes. It was observed that older generation aged between 50-60 mainly *Mahaguru* watched television while lying down on their *dewan* (bed) available in living room they called it hall as it was the most relaxing moment for them, as retired from their outside work. However middle age respondent between the age group 40-50 called *guru*sit on sofa or chair to watch their favourite programs, andyounger respondent aged between 30-40 *chelas* prefer to take seat in-front on groundwhile watching along with other; they often used to comment in between to give their instant responses and always disturb elders by asking questions related to programs. However, this structure (and hierarchy) in sitting arrangements vary from gharana to gharana and not only depend on the condition of availability of single television set. Perhaps sometime this hierarchy was also followed in the gharana where more one television sets are available as some chela's say they follow the hierarchy to obey and to gave respects to their mahaguru and guru.Young chela respondent gave their commentary and tried to elaborate their ideas about programming to their elder guru's. This direction reflects the dilution of authority and more liberty to talk in front of elder members. Every memberof the gharana utilizes their chance to talk about their experience about television. Specifically, young respondents seemed happy and very active in these discussions; such freedom in relations were not seen in earlier accounts of television watching in studies by Mankekar (1993) or Gupta (2000).

Television was found to be central in the life of many trans-respondent. It seemed to provide the comfort of everyday gathering in the gharana particularly in living area where all themember used to watch television, sometime with other members and sometime alone. Many respondents said that now there are fewer conflicts over issues (such as watching decisions, remote control, watching timing) because all of them have different routines and are busy with some other medium at the same time. In some responses it was observed that some single television set create the situations of inter-generational conflicts regarding programme choices between younger and older generation transgender members; and that younger generation members dominated over older generations in such programming choices and power relations in television watching.A sense of powerlessness was also felt by some respondents when it comes to exerting their viewing choices in thegharana domain. It was observed that for watching mythologicalprogramme manyelder transgender respondents had experienced a sense of powerlessness and domination. Thus, availability of different mediated medium gave choices that seemed to thus help members in gharana to overcome generational conflicts.

Transgender mediated representations V/S Men and Women opinion

Many men respondent believes that it is fair to consider a transgender person as a disorder in the society. However,some women respondent relates the issue with the feeling of motherhood and say they should not as they believe that they are also born with the similar procedure and each mother gone through a similar pain during the child birth so how we can consider them as a disorder for the mistake for that they are not responsible. Recalling their name many men claimed of calling and remembering them with Chakkaa,Hijra and Kinnar while women recall them with Hijra very few people recall them as transgender or ask for their name. Majority of respondents think that the transgenders have the power to bless others. Study says that most of the respondent think that the transgenders should be given equal opportunities in income, education& employment sectors.Most of the respondent have agreed that they have misbehaved with the transgenders once in their life. Mainly women respondent think that they are afraid of transgender people as they believe that the transgender person has the power to curse others while others were neutral on the subject. Within these negative responses there were also some categories of respondents who come forward to support the transgender people if they want to be the part of their society as they believe these people also need a fair chance to live a normal life that defiantly would not begin with marital status, womanhood etc.

On other hand many men and women think that yes mediated representations of transgender people are related to their realities as they say that this is how mostly transgender people look like, their voice or they react and the way they work, walk and behave in real life. These images are truthful portrayal of their mannerism as they say till now, we have not seen a transgender as an entrepreneur, doctor, teacher, driver, tailor, helper etc. Men and women claimed that if media will change their representation in any positive way and showcased them in a better role and positions then may there will be possibilities that when transgender people see these changing images their identities and professional roles in realities will also leads toward changes. It seems from these conversations that both transgender and people (men and women) in society need a change in content as a platform for issues of reflection of everyday struggles of marginalised group in a positive way.

Conclusion

Every transgender respondent has a unique and diverse responses for the use of media content some develop emotional relationship with the content while for some a leisure time activity performed to entertain themselves and to derive pleasure. It was found that the viewing pattern were mostly private channels dominated. Access to mediated medium, (such as television, internet) availability of gadgets (mobile, television sets)what to use, where to access, for them is a matter of taste, need and entertainment. Contemporary media representations are different for them in many ways as sometime some representations are also useful in shifting lifestyles.

The theme and subjects of transgender people in mediated representation are very less in numbers it also does notallow spaces to the aspects of everyday social realities of transgender people.

On other hand many men and women considering transgenders people as a disorder for society as they believe that they do no have a chance to live liberal life like them as their gender identities were not clear on some such basis, they cannot live a normal life that required societal possessions such as marital status,womanhood qualities, family etc to survive. However, some believe that they are incarnation of God and have a faith that transgenders are gifted with a power to cure and bless people.Many believe that mediated representations of transgender people are similar to their realities and possibly these representations have no useful for their community in shifting life chances in any ways.

Endnotes:

[1]Therefore, viewers exposed to 'racialized' elements result in reinforcing negative attitudes about racial minorities (Gilliam Jr and Iyengar 2000:561)

[2]Therefore, viewers exposed to 'racialized' elements result in reinforcing negative attitudes about racial minorities (Gilliam Jr and Iyengar 2000:561)

[3]Transgender respondents say many members in Gharana are working so their watching timing do not match with each other that gave them possibilities of watching television privately.

References

Afshana , S., & Din, H. (2017). Portraying Third Gender: A study of select Bollywood Movies. *International Journal of Interdisciplinary and Multidisciplinary Studies (IJIMS)*, 4(3), 60-68. Retrieved from www.IJIMS.com

Bhattacharjee, J. (2014). Third Gender in Indian Films with a special Reflection on Chitrangada. *International Journal of Scientific and Research Publications, 4*(12), 1-3. Retrieved from www.ijsrf.org

Chaudhary, P. (2019). Stereotypical Representation of Marginalised Transgender Characters in Indian Canon . *International Conference on Recent Trends in Humanities, Education, Arts, Culture, Languages, Literature, Philosophy, Religion, Gender and Management Studies (HEALM-2019)*, (pp. 102-104).

Clinard, M. B. (1967). *Slums and Community Development: Experiments in Self Help*. The Free Press, A Division of The Macmillan Company.

Gerbner George, L. G. (1985). *Living with Television: The Dynamics of the Cultivation Process* . Taylor and Francis.

Gupta, N. (2000). Just Switch off! Television: Creating the "Modern" Woman. *Social Scientist, Vol 28*(No 3/4), pp. 61-70. Retrieved August 19, 2014, from http://www.jstor.org/stable/3518190

Hall Stuart, D. H. (Ed.). (1980). *Culture, Media, Language Working Papers in Cultural Studies, 1972–79.* Academic Division of Unwin Hyman (Publishers) Ltd.

Jain, T. (2015). (Mis) representation of transgender in popular media. Retrieved from https:// feminisminindia.com/2015/12/09/ hijramediarepresentation/

Jobe, J. N. (2013). Transgender Representation in the Media. *Encompass,* 1-32. Retrieved from https://encompass.eku.edu/honors_theses

Johnson, K. (2005, January- April). Globalisation at the Crossroads of Tradition and Modernity in Rural India. *Sociological Bulletin, Vol 54*(No 1), 40-58. Retrieved 07 02, 2015, from http://www.jstor.org/stable/23620584

Mankekar, P. (1993, August). National Texts and Gendered Lives: An Ethnography of Television Viewers in a North Indian City. *American Ethnologist, Vol. 20*(No. 3), pp. 543-563. Retrieved August 19, 2014 , from http://www.jstor.org/stable/646641

McLaren, J. T. (2018). "Recognize Me": An Analysis of Transgender Media Representation. *University of Windsor Scholarship at Uwindsor*, 1-121. Retrieved from https://scholar.uwindsor.ca/major-papers

Mushtaq, T., & Ahmed, D. (2019). Third Gender Portrayal in Bollywood: An Analysis of Sadak. *International Journal of Trend in Scientific Research and Development (IJTSRD), 3*(3), 17-22. Retrieved from www.ijtsrd.com

Poole, R. J. (2017). European journal of American studies. *Towards a Queer Futurity: New Trans Television, 12*(2), 1-24. doi:10.4000/ejas.12093

Reitz, N. (2017). The Representation of Trans Women in Film and Television. *Cinesthesia, 7*(1), 1-7. Retrieved from https://scholarworks.gvsu.edu/cine

Yogi, R. K., Deepika, & Chaudhary, S. (2022, March 24-25). Shodh Shikhar 2022. *Discrimination Through Communication: In Special Reference of Transgender Society*, 154. Bhopal: Rabindra Nath Tagore University .

CHAPTER ELEVEN

A STUDY OF REPRESENTATION OF AN EFFEMINATE CHARACTER IN TAMIL CINEMA Priyanga.A

1.Introduction:

In this contemporary period, Tamil cinema plays a vital part in Indian cinema. Cinema undoubtedly defines the character and popularizing it to the people. Cinema has a huge influence in the society. Film characters are a major source of opinion of creation and have the strong influence on the attitude and mind-set of populace. Thus predominantly cinema shows men as a main character. Mainly the male protagonist and the male antagonist follow the masculinity character structure according to the culture and context. While the male character in Tamil films having the qualities of stereotypical male gender. There is always a connection between Tamil cinema and Tamil society. This makes to have many followers as fans for the certain lead actors for their masculinity in on screen. Film shows masculinity as power. In some rare films, Tamil cinema give effeminacy to the top actors who act in the film as either protagonist or antagonist.

This novelty was laudable but the worth of portraying the effeminacy to the character is still in question. Even the well famed actors handling the effeminacy and depict it with blithering by knowingly or by unknowingly. It is being questionable one for their gender through the gesture or dialogues of further characters in the selected Tamil films. This study tries to find how the effeminate characters portrayed in Tamil cinema?, why the female mannerism in man mocked?, why the gender of the character is being questioned in the films through the dialogues or gesture?. These questions were seeks answers through this study.

2.Effeminate:

Effeminacy is a feminine behaviour or mannerism embodiment with men rather than the traditional mannerism or behaviour or masculine of men. The word effeminate or effeminacy comes from Latin language which means "Womanish". This term usually means insult. The term first coined in 15th century as effeminate person.The characteristics of women which said intheculture as weak, soft, fragile and as an unmanly degree. Even in the contemporary days, people wouldn't get correct context about the term and misapprehension about their gender identity.

"Her father eager to change his effeminate child's way,would drag the child to boxing matches". Frances Robler, New York times, 20th October, 2020. The deviation of character or behaviour or .mannerism or style decides the gender and wither they are heterosexual or homosexual.

Before all the term androgynous is more vital to realize the gender expression of a person. Androgynous is an umbrella term which consist of both manly (masculine) women or effeminate men. Manly (masculine) women are having the masculine behaviour or character according to the context with female embodiment.

3.Review of literature:

While studying about the gender, a YouTube video by Maya in the channel of Maya's amma, shows gender is not a point to point thing. It is spectrum which consist of ore genders. She shows the gender as continuity spectrum with 4 rainbow bars. From this effeminacy comes under androgynous. This androgynous will be in both men and women who was belongs to specific gender with alternative gender expression.

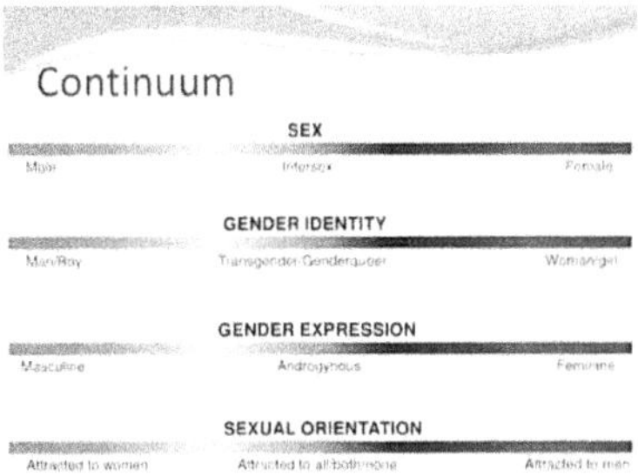

Enter Caption

Male –Long hair, feminine voice, elegance in walk, woman costumes, etc,.

Female –short hair, men costumes, muscle building, masculine voice, etc,.

These behaviours and mannerism will never decide one's gender. This nature will never been a chance to bully a person. Gender expression will never decide anyone's gender, it's about their wish.

For this study, encyclopaediashows the clear note about effeminate men and manly (masculine) women. This websites gives the history of the term and differentiation of androgynous between men and women.

Some news articles and feature article shows how the top actors handle effeminacy characters and how the importance of their acting lifts up the effeminacy among the audience. This article also shows how the plot wrongly handled the gender. To prove their gender women is being prey in the most of the films.

4.Research Methodology:

This research uses qualitative method to study how the effeminate characters are portrayed and being questioned about their gender for their feminine behaviour. This study uses content analysis to identify and to interpret the portrayal of effeminate characters in selected Tamil cinema. I have taken some selected films as primary data and other articles, news articles and YouTube videos as secondary data for this study. Content analysis is a study of process of scrutinizing the selected audio, video, text and gestures and their structure to ascertain the concept to find out the conclusion. Content analysis is an apt method for this study. In addition, this type of method can be applied while analyzing written text such as news stories, books, speeches, annual reports and others whether in analogue or digital form, in addition to audio visual content (Kripendorf, 2004).

4.1 Statement of the problem:

In simple term, people would have thought that the gender for human being is either make or female. But gender is a spectrum. In this spectrum, we have more than ten genders. Male and female are considered to be end to end while others will locate within the spectrum. This society considered and specifies their genders only according to their birth organs. Gender will never identify according to their sex organs. It can be identified through their birth organs, through their gender identity, through their expression, through their sexual orientation. But people only decide the gender by their sex organ only. They all decide the genderby their body. They never consider their mind. Beyond this people are getting influenced by cinema where cinema figures the gender by the mannerism and behaviour. The films are showing the male characters as strong, hard and bold to face anything and walk with straight face. Films are not ready to show their gender as spectrum. If the male person with female mannerism or behaviour, story and the other characters in the film trying to mock the personality or endeavour them to prove their gender as male. This gesture influence people to follow up the same in their real life.

4.2 Objectives of the Research:

- To analyze how the effeminate character showcased in the selected Tamil films.
- To scrutinize why the gender is questionable to the effeminate characters.
- To examine how these characters prove their gender.
- To analyze how films influence people to look up the people.

4.3 Sampling:

The leading actors in Tamil film industry who acted as an effeminate character in the films are as either protagonist or antagonist in throughout the film. These films were chosen from the Tamil films.Selected movies for the study and the effeminate characters in the films:Bhagavan fromAadhiBhagavan, Walter vanangamudi from Avan Ivan, Shiva Shankar from Varalaru and Love fromIrumugan movie. Top heroes like Jeyam Ravi, Vishal, Ajithkumar and Vikramplayed these roles.

5. Data Analysis and Interpretation:

The data analysis and the interpretation of this study has been given below with the comparison of each films.

5.1 Basic details about the film and character:

Table 1

SI.No.	Film name	Cast name	Role	Job of the character
1.	Varalaru (2006)	Shiva Shankar	Protagonist	Bharatnatyam dancer.
2.	Avan Ivan (2011)	Walter Vanangamudi	Protagonist	Thief and Folklore artist
3.	AadhiBhagavan (2013)	Bhagavan	Antagonist	Gangster
4.	Irumugan(2016)	Love	Antagonist	Criminal scientist

Table 1

The above table gives the basic details of the film and the effeminate character in the selected film with their job roles. The upcoming tables will show the characterization and the action done to prove their gender in the film will be shown.

5.2 Analysed information about thecharacters:

Sl.No.	Representation	Varalaru
1.	Framing	• Young, soft, kind and elegant dancer. • Feminine body language.
2.	Physical appearance	• Masculine with feminine behaviour due to classical dance.
3.	Costumes and Makeup	• Bharatanatyam costume and make up. • Men costumes and masculine makeup and outlook.
4.	Action took to prove the gender.	• Raping the female character called Gayathri.
5.	Gesture by other characters	• Mocking the personality by saying unfit for marriage. • Questioning the gender because of mannerism.

Table 2.1

Sl.No.	Representation	Avan Ivan
1.	Framing	• Young, aspiring folklore artist and a dancer. • Bold, strong and elegance sometimes. • Effeminate and masculine.
2.	Physical appearance	• Effeminate. • Muscle buildup. • Feminine voice(somewhere).
3.	Costumes and Makeup	• Men costumes and masculine makeup and outlook.
4.	Action took to prove the gender.	• Showing body power and fight sequence.
5.	Gesture by other characters	• Mocking the personality by calling sister and questioning the gender.

Table 2.2

Sl.No.	Representation	AdhiBhagavan
1.	Framing	• Young Gangster. • Bold, strong and cunning. • Effeminate and masculine.
2.	Physical appearance	• Effeminate. • Feminine voice.
3.	Costumes and Makeup	• Men costumes . • Feminine makeup and western outfits.
4.	Action took to prove the gender.	• Action sequence.
5.	Gesture by other characters	• Mocking the personality by calling him as woman for his behaviour and questioning the gender to took over his girl friend.

Table 2.3

Sl.No.	Representation	IruMugan
1.	Framing	• Cunning. • Bold and strong. • Effeminate and masculine.
2.	Physical appearance	• Masculine with feminine behaviour. • Masculine voice.
3.	Costumes and Makeup	• Men and women western costumes . • Female makeup.
4.	Action took to prove the gender.	-
5.	Gesture by other characters	• Mocking the character by showing sarcastic gesture.

Table 2.4

Interpretation:
Movie Name: Varalaru.
Character Name: Shiva Shankar.

Characterization:

Shiva - a young classical dancer who is ready to get married soon. Find a girlGayathri for marriage. Unfortunately she stops the marriage on the wedding day for Shiva's effeminacy because of his classical dance. She questions his gender for his effeminate character. This makes Shiva's mother to die. This makes Shiva to took revenge against Gayathri and he sexually assault her to prove his masculine gender.

Movie Name: Avan Ivan

Character Name: Walter Vanangamudi

Characterization:

Walter, an aspiring folklore artist. His dancing passion and acting sense makes him to carry effeminacy in his behaviour. This make him to mock by the step brother by calling him as sister for his mannerism. Whenever Saamy call him as sister, he would show his muscle power to him. One fine day, Walter got a chance to showcase his talent in front of a big star. This makes Saamy to realize his mistake.

Movie Name: AdhiBhagavan

Character Name: Bhagavan

Characterization:

Bhagavan, a cunning Gangster living in Mumbai with his girl friend. A young man from well settled family asking Bhagavan'sgirl friend to leave him because of his effeminacy.He mock Bhagavan for his feminine behaviour and questioning his gender.

Movie Name: IruMugan

Character Name: Love

Characterization:

Love, a mad scientist who is trying to defeat protagonist. During this sequence, he dress up like woman and walk across two police men. They mock and givingflirty expression. Beyond this, not any further characters questions the gender of Love through any gesture.

Findings:

- Film are reflection of people and influencing the people for treating the androgynous people.
- Gender is being questioned and treated by their behaviour and mannerism.
- Gender is a spectrum which consist of more than ten genders.
- Feminine is not in the behaviour, it is a mind set.

- Male can have feminine which doesn't decide his sex.
- Androgynous people are still bullied by the society.
- Gender expression will never be the same to men or women,it will be based on their wish.
- Character will be lethargic until it comes to gender. They have to prove them as men. This is also a mind set of patriarchy.
- To prove their masculine either they show their muscle power or virility.
- Women is being encountered to prove their gender.
- This study identified that films showcasing men and they need to be masculine. If effeminacy is found in the male character they will be mock and bullied through the dialogues and gestures.

Conclusion:

From this study, the effeminate characters are being bullied. Even the big stars plays the role, they treat effeminacy in a bad way. By the female gaze, men should be admired by only having the masculinity. If the men have elegance, soft, kind and other feminine behaviour which makes the audience to feel him as female or else having doubt in their gender. But really it is a androgynous expression where even female have the manly nature. It is nature and not a thing to bully.

Reference:

Krippendorff, K. (2004). Reliability in content analysis: Some common misconceptions and recommendations. Human communication research.

"Effeminacy ." Encyclopedia of Sex and Gender: Culture Society History. . Retrieved from Encyclopedia.com:

McGann, PJ. 1999. "Skirting the Gender Normal Divide: A Tomboy Life Story." In Women's

Untold Stories: Breaking Silence, Talking Back, Voicing Complexity, ed. Mary Romero and

Abigail J. Stewart. New York: Routledge.

Encyclopedia of Sex and Gender: Culture Society History. . Retrieved from

Encyclopedia.com

MEDIA AND GENDER : THE REPRESENTATION OF THIRD GENDER Prachi Malhotra andMehak Jonjua

INTRODUCTION

The basic idea of any media is awareness. In country like ours Cinema , specially Hindi Cinema aka"Bollywood " is one of the mediums of communication which influences our masses to such an extent that people change their life goals . Hero worship and Character influence is so profound that changes the life courses. This is the power of cinema. Our country is largely homophobic and there is a prevalent hatred for LGBT + Community. In this umbrella the most hated and ostracized community is that of TRANSGENDERS who by law are now credited as THIRD GENDER. Trans depictions in movies started with their characters being portrayed as comical, transvestite, villainous and scary. The masses who already were oblivious to their very existent, viewed them with further remorse and hatred.This study will analyze few movies of 20th and 21st century and see the changing dynamics w.r.t representation of transgender /bodies in Hindi movies.

RATIONALE OF THE STUDY

With media as a medium the lost respect of third gender can be revived .Cinema can help a great deal in overcoming the transphobia and help this ostracized community to be part of the mainstream if they are portrayed in right light with meaningful and responsible cinema.

OBJECTIVES

To study the gradual shift in movies where transgenders are showcased beyond comic or villainous characters and awareness about third genders within general masses.

RESEARCH QUESTIONS

1.Howtransgenders are portayed by our filmmakers ?

2.What is the impact of this portrayal on the audience and how they perceive this third gender ?

3.Is there any transition from 20th to 21st century movies where a food for thought is given to the audience about transgenders –to accept or reject them ?

RESEARCH METHODOLOGY

	RESEARCH METHODOLOGY
Content Analysis	It is a systematic analysis of texts.
The Universe	Bollywood movies produced/released between (Time span—1996-2021)
Sampling	Purposive sampling method-(Non Probability sampling)
Movies	Basis the presence of transgender characters that included "Darmiyaan,, Sangharsh, B.A Pass, Rajjo, Shabnammausi, laxmi,Tamana, Quissa, Chandigarh KareAshqui.
Unit of Analysis	Trans character Portrayal---Stereotype/Non-Stereotype
	Visual representation of trans bodies--) Unfitted and covered dresses, appropriate make-up and jewelry Fitted, cleavage, uncovered outfits, loud make-up and jewelry
	Standing ---- Comic, Professional, educated social worker, strong Prostitute, beggars, seductive dancers and criminal.

Enter Caption

ANALYSIS AND FINDINGS

Trans community is not presented positively in Bollywood movies. Most of the movies have "Mis-Use" their gender either in humor or villainous characters. But some of the movies of 90's like Tamanna, Darmiyaan and Shabnam mausi portrayed the Trans characters in good light that highlighted the plight of this community. But these movies were overshadowed by "Sangharsh " and" Sadak " where the villainous and negative characters were played by most talented actors with power full performances that even today audience remember them . But, with changing times and various platforms film producers/Directors esp. youth are taking up challenging social issues and awaring the audience.Bold issues of LGBT community is being communicated by many films , though the commercial success is not very high but awareness and audience likelihood has increased.'Chandigarh kare ashqui" (2021)has touched all issues related to transgender, social acceptance to self-acceptance. The movie clearly defines various questions related to transgenders which comes across the mind of a layman.This is the best part of the movie where difference between cisgenders/transgenders/transsexual is made very clear to the audience .Breaking the stereo type a trans woman is the lead in the movie. The shift is there but very marginal .This is one Bollywood movie released after so many years with this bold topic of third gender.

A small survey with randomsample of 100 individuals (aged 18-55) was done who watched "Chandigarh kare ashiqui" and the findings were quite surprising as:

1. Almost 90%of the respondents did not know who transgenders are as many confused them with LGBQ.
2. 20 % of the respondents were of the opinion that if more movies like this with logic and positive message is showcased then more awareness and thus acceptance of this community is plausible.

1. India being a homophobic nation 80 % said that acceptance will be extremely gradual and may take years for them to lead a "Normal" life.

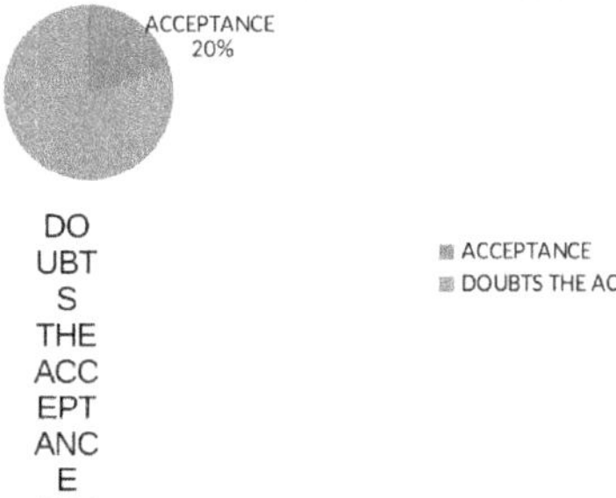

Enter Caption

CONCLUSION

Responsible cinema can definitely change the people's perception about third genders. Tillnow mostof theTransportrayal in movies is comic or negative. Some movies showcase their plight and raise empathy among audience. Idea is not to gain sympathy or hatred but equality. Bollywood has a mass appeal and filmmakers should support the cause of bringing the third gender to equality status. Awareness and Acceptance in right light should be the agenda in movies. Mass sensitization is important and media has the power to bring transgenders back in mainstream.

References

J. Bhattacharjee (2014). The third gender in Indian cinema, with a focus on Chitrangada. 4th edition of the International Journal of Scientific and Research Publications (12). http://www.ijsrp.org/research-paper-1214/ijsrp-p3695.pdf

Jain, T. (2015).Popular media's (mis)representation of transgender people.Jobe, J. N. https:// feminisminindia.com/2015/12/09/hijramediarepresentation/ (2013).

D. Mandeep and A. Raina (2015). Rudra's identity crisis in 'chitrangada': is she a technical woman or a natural man? 20(2), 60-68 in Journal of Humanities and Social Science. http://iosrjournals.org/iosr-jhss/papers/Vol20-issue2/Version-2/L020226068.pdf

Panda, N. (2016).The representation of the third gender in Bollywood films, 5 (1). http://www.drishtithesight.com/index.php/drishti/article/view/6

REEL MERGING INTO REAL: A STUDY OF MEDIA INDUCED HYPER-REALITY AMONG UNIVERSITY STUDENTS Chitralekha Agrawal and Dr Sayan Dey

Introduction:

As social psychologist Albert Bandura (1971) defines it, our environment plays key role in the learning of a person. Responses to a stimuli and cognitive concepts are learnt through observation, modeling and imitation of the behaviors, and the attitudes and actions of those who surround us.We are all surrounded by the media nowadays. Along with traditional media platforms, the web-enabled social media which can be accessed via mobiles phones anytime and anywhere is popular among Indians of all ages, particularly youths. A 2022Statistastudy finds out that in India, the number of people who regularly use smart phones for web surfing is 624 million. And, interestingly 448 million people out of them are active on some type of online social media platform.The percentage of Indian youth that use social media to gain knowledge and find social acceptance on a regular basis is 62 percent(Indiafacts.in, 2022). They study and learn through social media which is a virtual hyper-real environment with standardized and homogenized global symbols. These symbols have become a part of popular culture and are used to express a facsimile of reality (Bansal, D. 2017). Social psychologist Henri Tajfel (1981) states that our self-concept, sentiments, and behaviors are all influenced by our social identity that we build with reference to the symbolic culture of social media. It expresses the contemporary customs of the hyper real virtual environment that tricks awareness into distancing itself from genuine emotional connection in favor of artificial simulations and continual replications of fundamentally empty appearances. Pleasure or delight is essentially acquired through mimicking and recreating a fictitious version of reality rather than experiencing it.Both social and personal effects of mediatised communication are deep that gradually cultivate certain beliefs, attitudes and motivations in the minds of receivers.

According to Baudrillard when the representation of facts becomes so authentic and real that the viewers start receiving it as reality, it is called a Hyper-real condition. The blend of actual and artificial symbols is so perfect in such situations, that people believe it to be true. Such condition blurs the lines between facts and fantasy. Then what remains is an amplified state of manufactured truths. Baudrillards named this artificial exaggerated hyper-real state as "Simulacra" that have no originals but their replicas. It starts with creating the imitations of the real objects and symbols that is called "simulation". Baudrillard states that in post modern culture,imaginary symbols and characters that are intentionally created by the media have replaced the reality and meanings.Simulacra and Simulation are well-known for its exploration of signs and symbols, as well as how they connect to contemporary society. Hyper-reality divides the signed order into four phases; the first is Reflection, which can be defined as a faithful copy or image of the fact or reality. The second phase is Mask, which is a perversion of reality in which the representation is not original and can thus be classified as an untrustworthy picture or replica. Illusion is the third phase; it is the absence of a deep reality; in this phase, the sign appears to be a faithful image or duplicate, but it is not original. And, the fourth step is known as a Pure Simulacrum or Representation, in which the simulacrum has no resemblance to reality.It is semiotic notion; a collection of signifiers and the production of symbols that symbolize something that does not exist in reality, such as Mickey Mouse and Disneyland. The current state of mediatised hyper-real symbols and signs create trade value for the receivers.

Perception of 'Self' can be understood with the explanation given by the prominent Humanist Psychologist Carl Rogers. He claims that 'Self' is built around three key components: The Ideal self is the first half of this concept, followed by one's vision of oneself- The Image, and finally self esteem, which is one's acceptance and likeness to oneself in comparison to others.

Positive Psychology students define notion of 'Happiness' as a state where one experiences positive feelings about oneself and life. It is attached with the belief that s/he is living a valuable and noteworthy life that is good as well as satisfying (Lyubomirsky. 2007). The concept of 'World' refers to the entire globe with all the living and non living objects. It is the existence of reality in one's environment.

The goal of this study is to see how hyper reality affects Indian youth's perceptions of self, happiness, and the world, and how much of that information is influenced by the hyper real social media that is heavily influenced by the consumer culture.The paper connotes 'effects' as the outcome of mediatisedculture and discovers, documents and states the *consequences* of those 'constructed' symbols on youth.

Review of Literature

A vast number of past researchers and official surveyors have studied the effects of symbolic communication on the various strata of society. Bathran. R. (2021) studied media habits of college students to conclude that the students across disciplines believe that the social media do influence their social understanding and knowledge of the world. Cusack and Kosnac (2017) write how hyper real media texts are dictating a global religion and sacred culture to people of different age groups and strata who use social media. Karim, Oyewande et al (2020) observed that the long-term use of social media had a harmful impact on users' health. It has physical, emotional, and psychological consequences. Depression was discovered to be one of the most common side effects. Vandana and Lenka (2013) reviewed various past studies to find out the materialistic effect of media on the children. They concluded that children receive materialistic symbols positively that increased materialism among them. Destriana, Pranawa et al (2020) studied the hyper-reality behind 'foodstagramming' phenomena on the young people of Surakarta in Indonesia. They came to the conclusion that Foodstagramming is a simulation designed to generate a specific image to symbolise social status and achieve reputation.Lakha,N. in her Master's thesis studied the hyper-reality of youth gangs shown in films; which symbols are used to create the reality of those gangs in movies and how they impact the thinking process of society and youth.

SBI general survey (Brand Equity, 2022) on Indian women revealed that the financial independence ranks among the top three priorities of them. The India Gen Z report from Snapchat and Crowd DNA (2022) gives information on generation-specific rising audience behaviors, trends, and their impact on society. This generation is supporting openness around the world, redefining online life as something that feels real, meaningful, and genuinely fun. The four specific areas that gen Z refer from social media include Identity, communication, commerce, and connections.

Many previous academics in India and elsewhere have looked at the many facets of hyper reality's effects on various age groups and socioeconomic communities. The study of the different facets of its impact on students is still in its early stages. There are numerous aspects to investigate. This research paper aims to investigate the most fundamental features of hyper reality's impact on youth cognition, such as their concept of self-image, happiness, and the world that have not been covered in totality in any of the previous studies.

Research Objectives: The aim of the research is to understand

1. The effect of simulated mediatized culture on university students.
2. Whether the hyper reality extends beyond the hypermedia and affect students' basic understanding of the world.
3. The features of major simulated symbols that have the highest trade value in the minds of youths.
4. How the traded symbols are related to their values.

Research Questions:

- How students define themselves and their happiness in the social media driven hyper real world?
- Which is the main source of their information regarding the world and environment?
- Which social media platforms students use the most and why?

- What have they learned from those platforms?
- How their understanding of the basic concepts like self, happiness, achievement & the world has been distorted, affected, homogenized and standardized by the consumer culture?

Methodology:

This is a descriptive exploratory study that used triangulation method for data collection. Both qualitative and quantitative research tools were used to collect the primary data. The study focused on undergraduate and graduate students at the Delhi University which is India's most prestigious educational institution and that educates students from all over the country primarily Bihar, Rajasthan, Uttar Pradesh, Madhya Pradesh, Haryana, Himachal Pradesh, Jammu and Kashmir, and Delhi itself. The populations comprise of the male and female students aged between 18-27 years hailing from the different states of India. All the respondents are fluent in both Hindi and English languages, which were utilized to collect primary data throughout qualitative and quantitative surveys.

Secondary data was gathered from psychologists' and researchers' literary and research works. As it was important to understand the students' knowledge of the core concepts to construct a survey questionnaire, qualitative methods were employed. A focus group discussion (FGD) was conducted with Delhi University undergraduate students to know their conceptual knowledge of research concerns. In-depth interviews with four students (2 males and 2 females) were also done to comprehend their perspectives. As the final phase of data collection, a questionnaire was created based on FGD & Interview results and mailed to the respondents to collect quantitative data that was further analyzed to achieve the research objectives.

Results and Analysis:

The qualitative data gathered from students, revealed following pieces of information pertaining to their source and perception of the core research concepts.

- All studentsadmitted interactive media platforms as their preferred mode of communication where they pursue news and entertainment programs such as movies, music, gaming, chatting, and other activities for an average of 4-6 hours a day. They have no other way of networking, learning, or broadening their understanding of the world. All of themregularly browsesocial media, news websites, and various individual YouTube channels to stay up with the news.

- YouTube, Spotify, Instagram, and OTT platforms like Hotstar, Amazon, and Netflix are among students'favoritesocial networks. They binge-watch shows for long periods and this time does not include extra 2-3 hours spent browsing the phone screen reflexivelyduring various routine activities, such as riding the metro, waiting in class, sitting idly, and doing other things.

- Respondents accepted that their knowledge of the world is based solely on what they read online. Only a few of them read newspapers or watch news channels to keep up with the latest events. They prefer to acquire their world knowledge through Google News, news websites, or other media organizations'media pages. ABP News, NDTV, and News Laundry are the most popular news websites. Some kids use YouTube to view videos about competitions, study IQ, and other topics.

- Many of the respondents consume certain serials, OTT shows, websites feeds and movies only because it is considered intellectual and cool to watch it.

- 'Personality' according to them, is how people judge them and it is an important element of life. They all agreed that social media has taught them how to portray themselves better and has had a significant impact on their lives, beauty, and intellectual objectives. It has also aided their personal development. They're all very conscious of their online image and concerned about what others think of them.

- Majority of the respondents are aware that they frequently perceive themselves through the eyes of others and incorrectly assess themselvesas per the standards that social media has imposed on the image of 'a person' in today's society. They adhere to those norms since it is the law of the land.

- Insecurity, Financial Constraints, Troubled Love Life, Productive, Always Happy, Overthinking, Professional Growth, Depression, Tension, Fear of Left Out (FOMO), Stress, Panic Attacks, Network of Friends, Popular, Consequences, Confidence level, Potential, Emotional Stability, Healthy Lifestyle are some of the most commonly used and voiced terms during FGD and Interviews.

- Terms like 'Financial security', 'freedom', and 'public recognition' are commonly used by the students to define happiness and accomplishments. Money, Wisdom, Power, Self-Growth, Celebrity

Status, Stability, and Beauty are among their chosen achievements.

- Some of them define success as mental peace, but they also recognize that the mental peace can only be obtained through a prosperous financial profession. They all aspire to be billionaires and live in luxury. Many students, in fact, see financial hardship as the greatest impediment to their happiness and success.

- They acknowledged that being with family and friends brings joy, but that the amount of time spent with family is decreasing gradually and they socialize mostly through apps like Whatsapp with their family members also.

- Their self-esteem is boosted by societal recognition. If they accomplish something that does not get them social recognition, It is a wasted skill. This is the reason;kids enjoy displaying their abilities on numerous social media sites.

- Most of them choose adjectives like Independent, Cool, Hot, Dependable, Determined, Humanistic, Chill, and Unique to describe themselves.

- Some of them believe that they chose a particular career route because their parents wanted them to. For some students, their fathers serve as role models while several students named popular figures like Paulo Coelho, Che Guevara, J Cole, and businessman Naval Ravikant as role models, while others named Paulo Coelho, Che Guevara, J Cole, and businessman Naval Ravikant.

- Most students have ideal life goals based on well known media quotes and celebrity statements (mostly foreign). For instance, a student expressed desire to live life according to TyrionLanninster's words from HBO series Game of Thrones: "I drink & I know things."

A questionnaire with 25 questions was prepared keeping all the above inputs from the students. It was sent to 100 students of Delhi University that include both Post Graduate &UnderGraduate students. A total of 95respondents attempted to fill the questionnaire but only 61 students completed it. 34 students dropped it midway. The analysis of the data has been done on the basis of those 61responses.

1. **Demographic details of the respondents:**

Gender	Males- 79%	Females- 21%
Age Group	18-23 years - 78%	24-27 Years - 22%
Course Group	Undergrads- 85%	Post grads - 15%

Demographic details of the respondents:

(Percentage values are in round figures)

2. **Media consumption Habits**

Preferred media	New Media Platforms: 67%	Traditional Media like Newspaper, TV, Radio - 33%	Other- 0
Access Tool	Phone- 85%	Tablet- 9%	Laptop- 6%
Time Spent on social Media daily	2-3 Hours – 36%	4-6 Hours – 52%	More than 6 Hours- 12%

(Percentage values are in round figures)

Media consumption Habits

3. Social Media usages preferences: Why do I use media-

Socializing with Friends	33.38%
Entertainment	30.25%
Gaming	12.5 %
Studies	12.5%
News	9.38%
Other	1.9%

Social Media usages preferences: Why do I use media-

1- The lessons from Social Media: This is what I am Learning from Social Media :

2- Define 'I': The Self Concept

- Which Adjective defines me best:

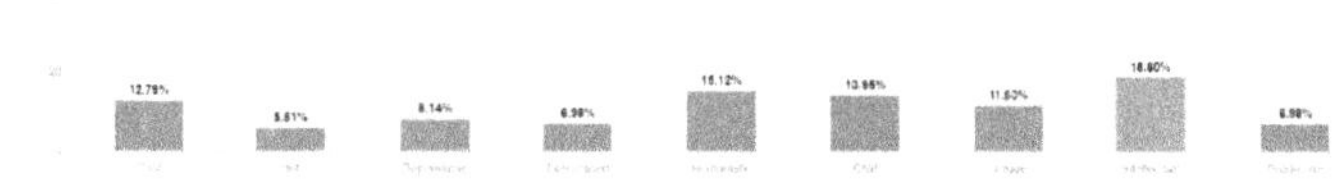

Enter Caption

3- My Personality: The positives & Negatives

- This gives me an edge over others:

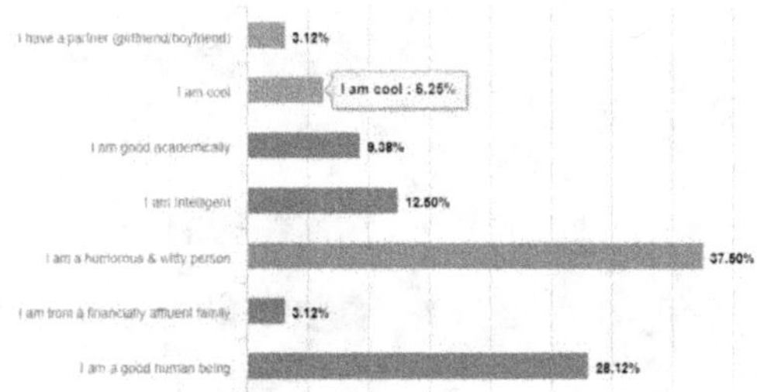

- This positive phrase fits me best:

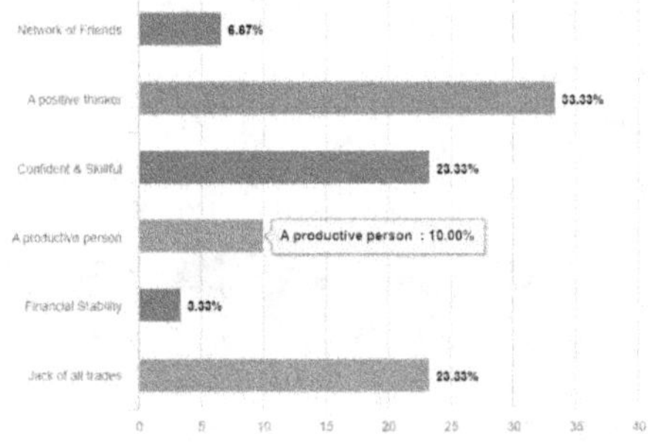

Enter Caption

- Negative side of me:

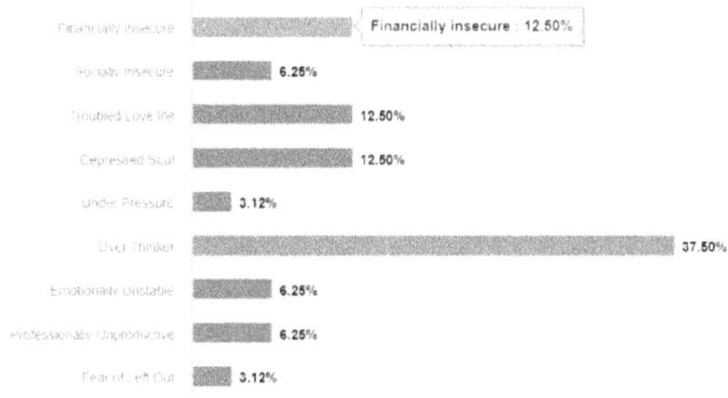

4- My Role Model

5- What makes me Happy: Concept of Happiness

- This boosts my self esteem:

Enter Caption

- The most important things to be happy and successful in life are:

Wisdom, Growth & Stability	28.12%
Money, Power & Status	21.88%
Health & Character	18.75%
Love &Peace of Mind	12.5%
Family & Friends	18.75%

- This is the biggest hurdle in path of happiness and success:

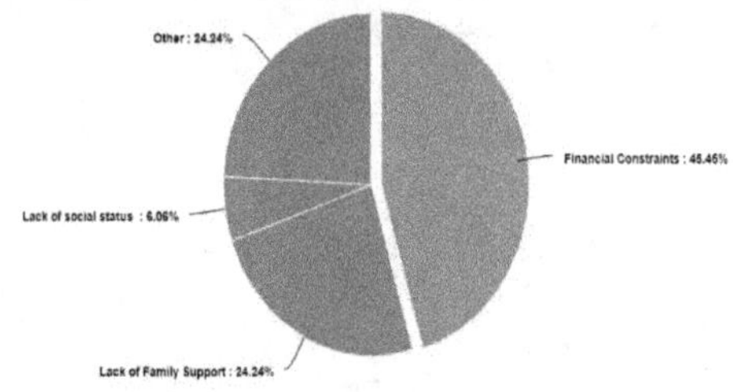

6- The Future Goals:

- Their 'Ideal' Future self:

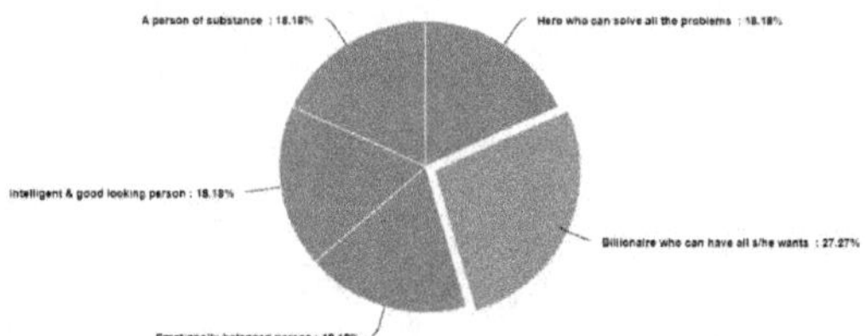

Enter Caption

- What They Want to Achieve:

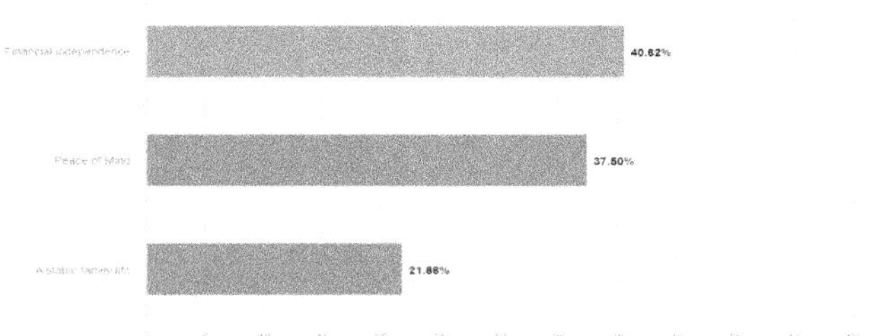

- In Society, they want to be regarded as:

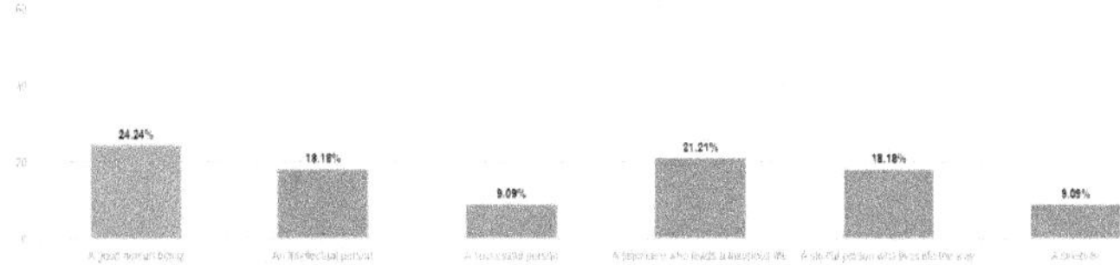

7- Concept of News: My understanding of world

- Which is my source of information regarding the world?

Enter Caption

- How often I post on social media regarding the contemporary word issues:

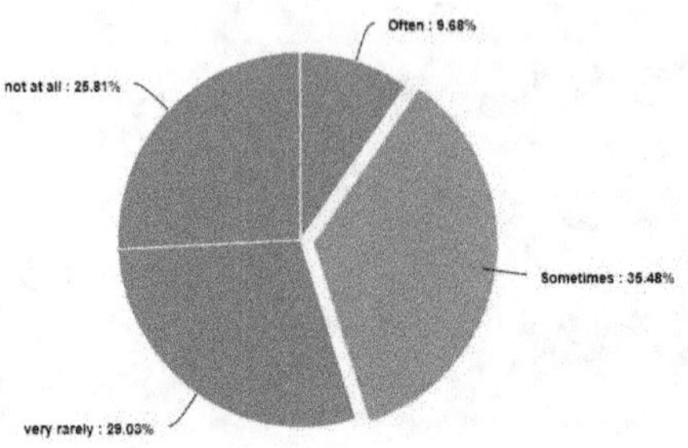

- Opinion regarding Ukraine-Russia War:

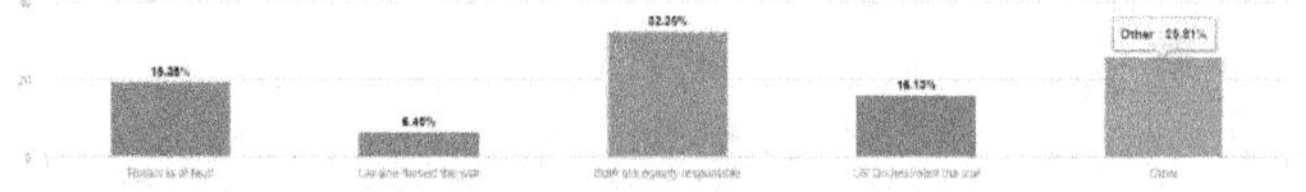

- What should be done to stop the war:

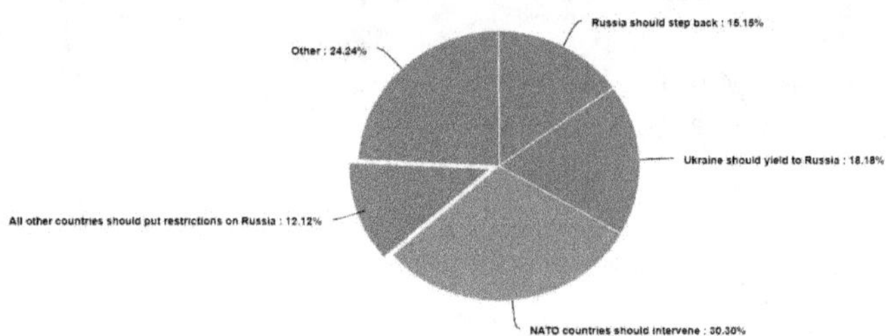

Enter Caption

- The war Implication according to me:

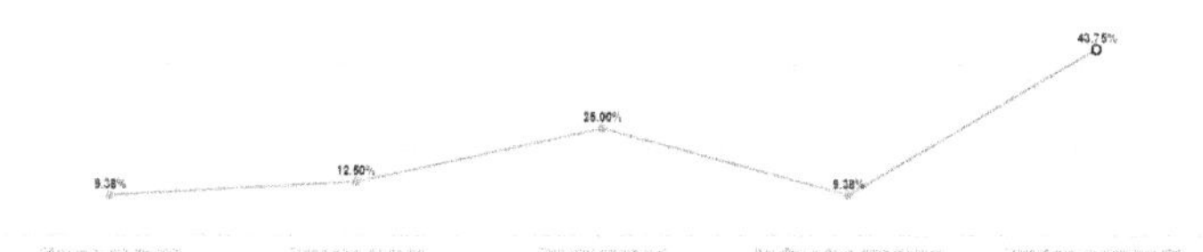

Enter Caption

Discussion:

The analysis of the responses reveals how most of the students surf internet daily for 4-6 hours,predominantly social media, with 85 percent accessing it via smart phone devices. It's an interesting discovery that also relates to students' widespread use of new media and their lower consumption of conventional platforms (33 percent). The trend shows how students are surrounded by web media, which creates a virtual environment in which they can learn and express themselves. It serves as a reference point for students as they learn and adjust their general behaviors as well as their social identities. The situation provides a hyper-real replica of cultural and social reality because the meditating environment uses symbolic symbols of high trade value. We may deduce facts from the results about how children are learning to express, adapt, and create themselves in accordance with consumer culture's homogeneous symbols and signifiers, which are regularly communicated by online communities. The media simulation of 'knowledge reservoirs' has a significant impact on not just their personalities, but also their perception of the world. A quarter of the respondents (24%) admitted that they use media to determine which studies and reference materials should be consumed in order to gain a better awareness of the world. This also entails a consistent selection of media signifiers. The preceding research findings provide solid evidence on their media consumption patterns and subsequent outcomes, clearly answering research questions 2, 3, and 4. Furthermore, the above findings back up previous study and statisticians' findings that the bulk of social media users consume it for news, entertainment,studies, connecting with friends, and drawing important symbolic conclusions that they later apply in their own lives.

The most intriguing conclusion is that the materialism has had a major impact on students who consider financial independence to be their top priority in life. As can be seen, 27.7% of respondents want to become a billionaire in their lifetime, while 21% want to be socially perceived as a billionaire who has everything they want. The majority of students (40 percent) choose financial freedom to peace of mind and life stability. Money, power, and status are the most important things to them in life. For them, monetary limits are not just the greatest hindrance to achievement, but also the source of their dissatisfaction. This could be attributed to the virtual media's capitalistic culture that affects students' thinking as they spend a substantial amount of time online. This is a significant result that helps achieve two research objectives by defining the key simulated symbols with highest trade values on media communities. **Money, luxury, and a pleasant lifestyle have become linked with**

happiness, success, and mental serenity. Their traded worth is consistent among communities, according to previous study conducted by researchers from other countries also. 'Money' is a hyper-real symbol for 'happiness.' Users of the media are led to believe that if they achieve financial independence, they will be content with their lives. 'Financial well being' is exchanged for 'happiness', while 'economic difficulty' is exchanged for 'despair and sadness'.

The students have a tremendous desire to be seen and admired. When they are recognized and appreciated, it boosts their self-esteem. It's no surprise that children want to be a jack of all trades or someone with a diverse skill set, as these qualities are highly prized in today's virtual society. Many students regard financial insecurity, a rocky love life, and a professionally unproductive attitude, among other things, to be negative aspects of their personality, and **a sizable percentage of respondents (12%) say they are depressed souls. The most shocking consequence of all is the over-thinking attitude of the students. 37% students deem themselves over thinkers and consider it a negative quality. Over thinking is an outcome that has been attributed to the extremely superficial virtual world by many psychologists and new media researchers in past studies.**

Another research goal is to investigate the extension of hyper-reality beyond hypermedia, which is accomplished through the recorded reactions, which demonstrate how respondents are similar in their perspectives on research issues. The information decodes the traded values of the most commonly used hyper-real symbols. **Professional un productivity is an exchanged value of failure, and skills and traits are traded for recognition, praise, and achievements. The use of networked platforms, where all gen Z users communicate in similar linguistic terms to identify themselves with one another, has also resulted in the emergence of many new phrases, words, and concepts. Their conceptions of key terms are similar, and their motivations, attitudes, logic, and beliefs are all influenced and created by semiotic media culture.**

The study's findings also highlight how university students get their world information from social media. They, on the other hand, only occasionally voice their views on current events on the same platforms. Only 9% of students said they frequently used social media to express their views on global issues. Though, in the context of the contemporary Ukraine-Russia conflict, their worldview is similar to what is being propagated in the international media. The majority of respondents holds Russia responsible for the conflict and feels NATO countries should intervene to bring it to an end. They all believe that the war has affected various countries' trade. **This conclusion shows that students rely on social communities and web feeds to create their political opinions, which could have major consequences for their home nation as well as the rest of the world. Users' perceptions are distorted by bogus media representations, which train people to respond in a similar fashion to a specific set of stimuli.**

The findings back up Bandura's hypothesis of environment-based vicarious learning of behaviors, attitudes, beliefs, and perceptions. It is clear that the younger generation has immersed themselves in the virtual world and is learning via it. They prefer to communicate utilizing the most common social media linguistic indicators that denote specific emotions and are widely used in the simulated virtual world. **With the help of a set of materialistic symbols, the meditized environment is establishing a congruent domain of phoney realities that is ending the originality of ideas and acts, demolishing actual meanings of essential concepts, and standardizing behaviors around the globe.**

Conclusion:

The findings reveal that the hyper real world of media, which is driven by consumer culture, has had a substantial impact on young brains' mental processes and understanding. **The most commonly used signifiers of happiness in popular culture, financial independence and monetary security, have been incorporated into their concept of the ideal self and happiness.** As they use media as a reference point for personality development and social behaviors, the simulation of reality has an impact on students' thinking processes and leads them to a symbolic unreal environment in which reality has been replaced by symbols that signify reality without any real references. As a result, **a generation of young people has been moulded by popular symbolic and materialistic culture in terms of worldview, beliefs, and attitudes.** Carl Rogers' three-part concept of self, which comprises ideal self, self image, and self esteem, sees consumer society as having dominance over them. **Students use money's exchange value to define all three aspects of themselves. The concept of happiness is also interpreted in the terms of monetary efficiency. Joy, happiness, positive well-being, have all been associated with the Hyper-real sign of financial strength. The findings support Baudrillard's beliefs**

in a postmodern civilization of simulations and simulacra, in which real-world concepts have been substituted by meticulously produced and exaggerated symbolic reel representations. Today's culture is evolving into a symbol-dominated civilization that expresses, acts, relies on, trades, and believes in media-induced symbolic gestures and illusions. This is a concerning symptom of a growing generation whose realities are twisted, with actual meanings being substituted by artificial, meditized symbols of popular culture that cause consumers to behave similarly.**The research study draws the conclusion that the manufactured hyper-real symbols of media do impact cognizance of those students who uses social media regularly for hours andtheir consciousness is profoundly influenced by the symbolic culture fostered by online communities. The effect is so strong that the students are unable to tell the difference between reality and fiction. They perceive, comprehend, and accept the world through the eyes of virtual reference groups.**

References:

Ahmad, N., Tekke, M.(2015).Rediscovering Roger's self Theory and personality.*Journal of Educational, Health and Community Psychology*, (4). ISSN: 2088-3129. Find at URL: file:///C:/Users/ADMIN/Desktop/3245-5959-1-SM.pdf

Bandura. Albert. (1971). Social Learning Theory. UK: Pearson Publicatons

Bansal, Dipika. (2017). Globalization of Consumer culture: An empirical survey of the consumers in Delhi. *Business Anlyst*, 38(1), 213-239.

Bathran, Radha (2021). Media Habits of Collage Students and the need for critical media literacy in India's higher education institutions.*Communicator,*LVI(4), 35-41

Baudrillard, J.(2006).Simulacra and Simulation. US: University of Michigan Press.

Brand Equity. (2022). *Financial independence ranked among top 3 priorities for women: SBI General stud.* Find at URL:https://brandequity.economictimes.indiatimes.com/news/research/financial-independence-ranked-among-top-3-priorities-for-women-sbi-general-study/90125880

Brand Equity. (2022). *AR is changing Indian GenZ's shopping behaviour: Snapchat report.* Find at URL: https://brandequity.economictimes.indiatimes.com/news/research/ar-is-changing-indian-genzs-shopping-behaviour-snapchat-report/90667053

Cusack, C.S., Kosnac, P. (Eds.). (2017). Fiction, Invention and Hyper-reality from Poular Culture to Religion. London: Routltdge

Destriana, N., Pranawa, S., Nurhadi, N. (2020).Foodstagramminghyperreality in consumption behavior in Indonesia.*HarmoniSosial: JurnalPendidikan,* 7(1), 85-95

Karim, F., Oyewande, A. et al (2020). Social Media Use and Its connection to mental health: A systematic review. *Cureus.*12(6).doi: 10.7759/cureus.8627

Lakha, Naima. (2020). *STRAIGHT OUTTA FILMS: A QUALITATIVE MEDIA ANALYSIS OF THE HYPERREALITIES OF YOUTH GANGS.* [Masters Thesis, Wilfrid Laurier University], Watrloo, Canada.

Lyubomirsky, S.(2007). The How of Happiness: A new Approach to getting the life you want. New York: Penguin Group.

Rogers, C. R. (1961). On Becoming a Person: A Therapist`s View of Psychotherapy. Boston: Houghton-Mifflin.

Statista Report. (2022). *Digital population across India as of February 2022.* Find at URL:https://www.statista.com/statistics/309866/india-digital-population/

Indiafacts.(2022). *Internet & Social Media Usage among youth in India: Mcafee Report.*

Tejfel, Henri. (1981). Human Groups and Social Categories. London: Cambridge University Press

Vandana, Lenka, U. (2013). A review on the role of media in increasing materialism among children.*Procedia-social and behavioral Science,* 133(2014), 456-464.

CHAPTER FOURTEEN

TO STUDY THE IMPACT OF DIGITAL MEDIA ON DIGITALLY ILLITERATE PEOPLE Anuj and Dr. Dheeraj Kumar

Introduction

Media has become a very essential part of life. People are connected with media directly or indirectly. Media is always considered a powerful tool. Media is divided in three formsi.e. New media, Electronic media and Print media. Newspapers, Books, Magazines and other printed material etc are including in Print Media. Electronic media came after the invention of Radio and Television.

The reach of radio & television is good. Electronic media's Radio is also very helpful for illiterate people.New after the indentation of the internet people connected technology with the internet. Now a day's new media is a very influential medium. New media is also a centre of attraction of all people.

The Internet is changing the world. Earlier banking was very complicated but after the emergence of UPI or net banking, it's a very easy task. Various banks are providing facilities of Know Your Customer in digital mode by video call verification. Earlier it was a very complicated and tough task people used to visit the bank with documents and used to wait in long queues.Most banks are trying to follow e-KYC. Education changed after the covid pandemic.Now people are aware that what is offline and online. It doesn't matter whether they are literate or not.

The various banking system, government schemes, and adhar-related work can't be completed without a one-time password (OTP). The government is launching day by day new schemes with their website.Governments also distribute laptops and tablets to citizens.

New media is very beneficial it is interactive and it save time and economy. Now reading habit of readers are changing because people are using ebooksthe help of electronic orators.Many virtual platforms are provinding books in audio format.After the pandemic films are also released on OTT platforms.

WEB 3.0 opens the door for interactive media. Now people easily interact with each other. Web 3.0 also opens the door to viral videos.In the post, modern era mobile has emerged as a very powerful tool for every person.

Digital media is equipped with a calculator for Artificial intelligence. Media is changing day by day according to the needs of users. It updates from time to time by both methods from hardware to software.The talkback feature is very good because it assists the blind and low vision.

New features in new media are adding day by day and these developments are in both field hardware and software. Now people travel with the help of Google maps. Google map is very helpful feature to find and search new places and it also predicts scientifically true predictions like time consumption of travelling and traffic and general people have basic rights of edit in Google mapimately time consumption during driving or walking, now an updated feature Google map shows a warning during above speed limit. Surveillance of Traffic violations are also conducted by digital media and fines are also paid with the help of digital media. Now telemedicine services are provided by health professionals to patients.

(Bejaković, 2020) stated that digitalization is not only the driver of economic growth but is one of the key factors influencing these positive changes.

According to census data, a person who is aged seven and above who can both read and write with understanding in any language is treated as literate. There is no need not to receive any formal education or acquire any minimum qualification to be treated as literate for a person (Census Report 2011).

The digital divide has existed between the various segments like educated and uneducated, economic classes, globally, and more and less industrially developed nations [Margaret Rouse, 2006]

Digital Literacy has been defined simply as awareness, skills, understanding, etc. to operate comfortably in Information Technology enabled environments (Anil, 2013).

The rationale of study

Digital media is helping a lot there is no doubt. digital media users can be divided into three types i) they use digital media they are updated ii) they use digital media but they are not familiar and iii) in this group there are two types of people iii. i) they are educated but they are not aware how to use media, iii.ii) they are illiterate they are not aware how to use digital media. Census data of 2011 shows that 74.04 % is the literacy rate of the country. Under the policy of E-governance, various facilities are online. Few services will be added in the coming days. Illiterate people face various difficulties. Some time government issues various schemes with last-date limitations. At that time various illiterate people pay the fee for services that are freely available by the government.

Literature review

Bhatnagar, H (2017). Demonetisation to digitization: A step toward progress find that demonetisation was good step taken by the government toward massive digital transformation of the country. Demonetization is a very basic element of a cashless economy and combating black money. The number of online baking frauds is increasing due to digitization. Various people digital media but they are not much familiar and also not much aware about security issues. People don't know how to use OTP.

Suresh, A. (2021). Stated that electronic banking is the hope of the future.New technologies are making banking an easy task. Nowadays scan or UPI is in trend. It sounds great because payment transactions have become now an easy task. New users or digitally illiterate people send money to the wrong account and face difficulty when receivers' payment gateway faces some technical glitch.

Sinha, P. (2021). Found that the Digital India mission was launched by Prime Minister NarendraModi on 1st July 2015 to upgrade the country into a digital empowered society and intellectual economy. Various steps have been taken by the government of under the Digital India campaign like Digilocker, UMANG, E-Hospitals, Epathshala, Bharat Interface for Money(BHIM), MyGov.in, eSign, and various government applications. The government has started various programs but people but there is a lack that how people will update. It's the responsibility of citizens how to use digital platforms.

Zende, S. (2021).Says that Digitalization is a process of converting information into a digital format.Digitalization is making our lifeless dependent and devoid of human interaction. Now all information is on our mobile phones. Digital illiteracy rate is high in town and villages. This is a new system so it's the responsibility of the citizens we will have to learn this technology. Cyber threat is increasing day by day and there are various type of crime like i'd or password to cyber terrorism but India is not only exception because cyber crime rate are increasing in all over the world.People are supporting Digital india initiative but we can't deny the risk of digital threats. Most people don't want to change according to time, they want to live traditionally.

Manoj, G. (2021) found that digital platforms are easy to use and cheaper. The government spends billions of rupees on the publication of currencies. The digital economy is good and it requires less cost on maintaining as compared to traditional economy methods. A cashless society is good in theories but practically in a cashless society, there is a threat of hacking and privacy issues. India is being prepared for cashless economy but there are various hindrances and we also know that India is heterogeneous society on various dimensions. Mandal, A (2022) stated that women represent 50 percent of the population. We live in a very world where everyone can access all the information, doesn't matter is false or true. Social media is a powerful tool but new media have also a dark side, especially for women. Also, suggest that regulated media will be helpful.

Mili, M &Duwarah, S (2021) found that Cash is very important for any economy. majority of poor people complete transactions in cash. all countries want to complete the transaction in a cashless system because of its basic infrastructure for a transparent economy and curb corruption. India is doing good in the field of digital payments.

Objectives of Research

- To study how illiterate people use digital media for personal use
- To study how illiterate people use digital media for government schemes
- To study how illiterate people use one-time password
- To study how they complete a task by digital media

Research Question

- How much illiterate people spends on E-services?
- How do they complete their online task?
- Which type of difficulty do they face?
- How do they decide trustworthy during OTP or banking services?
- How do illiterate youth use digital media?
- How do they complete (UPI) Unified Payments Interface?

Research Methodology

To find out the answers to the research question and find the solution objective mixed-method research has been used. According to the topic, this study was based on a cross-sectional study.

Type of data: Primary data

Area of Study: South Delhi

Target Audience: Illiterate people of South Delhi

Sample size: 100

Sampling frame: Illiterate people more than 18 years old

Sample selection method: Non-probability method

The subtype of sample selection method: Purposive method

Data collection tool: Schedule

Analysis and findings

Q1. Do you use your mobile phone for calls or accessing the internet? Please tell me all that you use. Phone calls Accessing the internet Both	
	Percent
Accessing the internet	14
Both	75
Phone Calls	11
Total	100

14 percent of respondents respond that they use the internet, 11 % say that they use the phone only for calls, rest 75% say that they use mobile phones for both calling and the internet.

Q2. Do you use any social networking or social media applications? Yes No	
	Percent
Yes	75
No	25
Total	100

25 percent of respondents don't use social media on mobile phones. 75 percent of respondents use social media.

Q3.(Ask If Q2= Yes) Which social media Platforms do you use? Please tell me all that you use. Facebook Whatsapp Twitter Instagram Youtube Other	
	Percent
	25
Facebook	8
Facebook, Whatsapp	13
Facebook, Whatsapp, Instagram	5
Facebook, Whatsapp, Instagram, Youtube	8
Facebook, Whatsapp, Youtube	21
Instagram	1
Twitter	5
Whatsapp	10
Youtube	4
Total	100

Enter Caption

21 percent of respondents have accounts on Facebook, WhatsApp, and youtube. 13 percent use Facebook and WhatsApp. 8 percent use Facebook, WhatsApp, Instagram, and youtube. 8 percent use Facebook. 10 percent use WhatsApp only. 5 percent use Twitter. 5 percent use Facebook, WhatsApp, and Instagram. 1 percent use only Instagram.

Q4. What would you say is your source of information about the new government schemes or policies? Family, friends, or neighbors Formal or Informal respresentatives Publicly owned television Private TV news channels Radio Newspapers Internet Social media/social networking sites Customer service centre Others	
	Percent
Customer service centre	23
Family, friends, or neighbors	34
Formal or Informal respresentatives	26
Internet	3
Newspapers	4
Private TV news channels	4
Publicly owned television stations / Doordarshan News	1
Radio	1
Social media/social networking sites	4
Total	100

34 percent of respondents say that they inform about new policies by their family, friend, and neighbors. 26 percent of respondents say that they get informed by formal or informal representatives. 23 percent say that they know about new policies from customer care centers. 4 percent say that they know from private news channels, and 4 percent responded that they know from newspapers. 1 percent known by radio and government channels.

Q5. Do you use online payment method Yes No Refused

Enter Caption

Don't Know	
	Percent
Yes	34
No	57
Refused	1
Don't Know	8
Total	100

57 respondents say that they never use an online payment method. 34 say that they use online payment methods. 1 percent of respondents don't want to reply to this question. 8 respondents were not aware of this method, they have only listened that transactions are completed by mobile.

Q6. (Ask If Q5= Yes), how you use One Time Password	
By yourself Family member Anyone Never use Refused Don't Know	
	Percent
	66
Anyone	1
By yourself	8
Family member	25
Total	100

25 respondents responded that they take the help of family members during online payments. 8 percent say that they complete it by themselves. 1 percent says that they take the help of anyone.

Q7. How do you complete your online work like government schemes, Aadhar card, hospital appointments, etc?
Do yourself Family Cyber Café Customer service centre Refused Don't Know

Enter Caption

	Percent
By yourself	4
Customer service centre	26
Cyber Café	30
Family	34
Don't know	6
Total	100

During general online services, 34 percent of respondents complete tasks with the help of family members. 30 percent of respondents go to cybercafes. 26 percent go to customer service centers. 6 percent of respondents don't know about it. 6 percent do it by themselves.

Q8. Have you faced threats during phone banking or OTP? Yes No Refused Don't Know	
	Percent
Yes	69
No	18
Don't know	13
Total	100

69 percent of respondents feel threat during OTP and banking-related calls. 18 percent don't feel fear. 13 percent of respondents don't know about OTP.

Q9. Have you tried to learn digital media (Social Media & UPI) Yes No Refused Don't Know	
	Percent
Yes	81
No	19
Total	100

81 percent of respondents responded. They have tried to learn media or UPI. 19 percent say that they never tried to learn these skills.

Enter Caption

Conclusion

Digital media is an essential tool in the postmodern era. Media is directly or indirectly associated with all dimensions of human life. The Internet has made life very easy because most of the services are available on the mobile phone. Mobile is nothing for those who are technically sound or who understand the basics of social media. Various services are available free on digital platforms. Some people are charging a high fee to digitally illiterate people in the name of service charge. Digital frauds are increasing day by day. Their easy targets are digitally illiterate people. Now the world is talking about artificial intelligence, but various people don't know the difference between login IDs and passwords.

References:-

Bhatnagar, H. (2017). Demonetization to Digitization: A step Toward Progress. *Management and Economic Research Journal,* 3, 11-15

Mandal, A. (2022).A study on the impact of social on women empowerment in India.*EPRA international journal of multidisciplinary research(IJMR).* 8(2), 168-170.

Manoj, G. (2021). The Digital Economy of India: Challenges and prospects. *Emperor journals of economic and social science research.*3(5), 166-170

Mili, M. &Duwarah, S. (2021). A study on the cashless economy in India: its benefits and challenges. *Indian journal of economics and business,* 20(3),1663-1670.

Suresh, A. & Rani, J. (2021). Barriers and challenges faced by consumers in the e-banking services sector in India. *International Journal of Global Business.*14(1), 13-24.

Sinha, P. (2021). Digital India: An overview, *International Journal of Advances in Engineering and Management.* 3(9), 806-809.

Zende, S. (2021).Digitalization in India prospects and challenges.*International Journal of Entrepreneurship & Technology.*29-31.

CHAPTER FIFTEEN

RADIO AS A SOURCE OF INFORMATION AND EDUCATION IN RURAL AREAS WITH ESPECIAL REFERENCE TO ARUNACHAL PRADESH

Champa Devi

1. Introduction

In today's modern society of new media technologies, radio still occupies a vital position especially in rural areas. The rural people still rely on radio to access information considering it as a cheap and portable medium of information, communication and education. Since the rural population is going through a process of transformation from traditional to modern, the participation of the indigenous people in radio programmes help them to explore their opinion in developmental process.

Situated in the easternmost part of India, Arunachal Pradesh is the largest state in Northeast region in terms of its land and forest. It is a home to about 26 major tribes with many other sub-tribes.The media landscape of the state comprises of folk media, newspapers, radio, television and films besides digital media and blogs. Out of the all these mass media, the rural people residing in far flung areas are mostly prefer radio to get different kinds of information, education and also for entertainment purpose. Radio being the least expensive mode of communication, has the ability to reach all corners of the globe. It has emerged as the most effective medium for development and public education, particularly in rural regions. It has the ability to influence individuals from all areas of life. Apart from informing and updating us, radio educates us about human rights and makes us aware of societal concerns and challenges. Wabwire(2013) writes radios assist people by encouraging expression and engagement, as well as valuing native customs, through providing access to information and stimulating economic growth. It functions as a vehicle for emphasizing the fundamental human rights of marginalized populations, and it has become the voice of the poor as well as silent, agricultural laborers and destitute indigenous people.

Television though occupies a better place in the life of rural populace but it depends on the availability of electricity supply.Moreover, the villagers can easily connect with the radio programmesbroadcast from All India Radio Itanagar and All India Radio Pasighat, which are based on their culture, traditions and information needs. And majority of the radio programmes are broadcast in local dialects besides Hindi and English languages to cater its target audience especially rural areas.Hence, radio becomes their primary source of information that help to create awareness on various social, cultural, economic as well as political issues of society. Radio also educate rural masses about their rights, facilities provided by the government to upgrade rural livelihood and about health, hygiene and sanitation.The study focused on AIR Itanagar and AIR Pasighatas a source of information and education for the tribal society in Arunachal Pradesh and its contribution in various aspects to bring growth in rural society.

1. Operational Definitions

I. **Radio:**In the study, radio refers to AIR Itanagar and AIR Pasighat and its various programmes and news updates being broadcast through All India Radio wave.

II. **Information and Education:**In the study, information and education refers to those information and radio programmesrelated to various issues of society such as lack of educational institutions, public health and hygiene, sanitation, gender inequality, safe drinking water, immunization or vaccination programmes, right to education, save the girl child, social campaign to eradicate drug menace, child labours, etc. that are being broadcast from radio to disseminate information and to educate rural masses.

III. **Rural Masses:** It refers to those villagers who have mostly depended on agriculture and other allied activities and doing small business for their livelihood.

3. Rational of the study

Radio broadcast various kinds of information on different issues of society for the rural masses and this might have influenced their day-to-day life. Since radio has been an important source of information and also educate the tribal society in Arunachal Pradesh, it might have contributed to bring growth in all aspects in rural areas. As the rural society in Arunachal Pradesh are witnessing speedy growth in all aspects of life, it becomes necessary to identify factors for the change in this tribal society. Hence, there is a need to do proper academic research and investigation in rural areas to find out the factors that influenced the rural society towards transformation. However, no serious attempts have been made to understand the potential of radio broadcasting for the growth of a society especially in rural areas.

The rationale of the study is to explore the role of AIR Itanagar and AIR Pasighatas a source of information and educating rural masses on various issues of society. It also explores the contribution of radio to bringing out growth in rural areasin various aspects. The findings of the study may help scholars, academicians and media professionals to understand the potential of radio broadcasting and how it helps to educate rural masses on various societal problems by disseminating information. It will also help governments to understand how traditional media like radio can contribute to developing rural areas.

4. Objectives

The primary objectives of the study are:

I. To identify different sources of information in rural areas of Arunachal Pradesh.

II. To explore the role of AIR Itanagar and AIR Pasighat in disseminating information and educating to rural masseson various issues of society.

5. **Research Questions**

I.   What are the different sources of information in rural areas of Arunachal Pradesh?
II. DoesAIR Itanagar and AIR Pasighathave any role in disseminating information and educating the rural masses on various issues of society?
III. Does radio help to contribute to bring growth in all aspects in rural areas of Arunachal Pradesh?

6. **Research Methodology**

The study focuses on the mass media exposure in rural areas and the role of AIR Itanagar and AIR Pasighatin disseminating information and educating educate rural masses on various issues of society. It was conducted in ten separate villages of East Siang and Papumpare districts of Arunachal Pradesh. The villages of East Siang districts are TakiLalung, Ngopok, Sibo, Rani and Ranging and the villages in Papumpare district are Bat, Ganga, Chimi, Mugli and Apop-Sango. A survey method was used for the collection of primary data while the secondary data were collected from various published or unpublished sources.

I. **Population and Sample**

A sample of 400 respondents from radio households was randomly selected from ten villages of Arunachal Pradesh. For the collection of primary data, an interview schedule was employed.The respondents were from different walks of life.

II. **Area of Study**

The study has been conducted in ten villages of two districts of Arunachal Pradesh. The area of the study is limited to two district- East Siang and Papum Pare where mostly the Adi and Nyishi indigenous people are residing. The rationale of selecting these two districts is that both have achieved different levels of modernizations. Also, the first radio station was established in East Siang district in 1966, there are maximum probability to witness speedy growth and development in the nearby rural areas, while on the other hand, the capital city Itanagar is located in Papumpare district, hence the probability to realize growth among the rural masses in the nearby villages are high. Hence, in this context, the role of radio as a source of information and education in rural areas are vital in this tribal society.

7. Findings and Analysis

Despite the availability of television, radio, internet connectivity and newspapers (few villages) in rural areas of Arunachal Pradesh, the people are active users of radio for accessing information, educational and also entertainment purpose. Though they owned television in their house and also access to internet connectivity but it depends on the regular electricity connection in the area.In remote villages where the access to other mass media was not possible, the rural people duly rely on radio programmes for any kind of information.

I. Profile of the respondents

The profile of the respondents outlines the characteristics of the population under the study. The researcher tries to analyse the social, cultural and economic background of the respondents in different geographical settings of rural areas. The survey covered 400 respondents from different professions, age groups and gender.

a. **Gender:** The respondents are classified based on the gender- Male and Female. Out of 400 respondents, 236 are male which constitute 59.0 percent of the total population and 164 are females which constitute 41.0 percent.

b. **Age:** The age of the respondents has been grouped in five sections i.e. 19-24, 25-34, 35-44, 45-54, 55 and above. The age group of 25-34 has the highest respondents which is followed by 45-54 age group. Based on the data, we can say that the youngsters and the middle age people resides in rural areas listen more to radio programmes for different kinds of information.

c. **Occupation:** As per the data, 37.3 percent respondents are engaged in farming or agricultural work and they acquired less educational qualification. This category occupies highest number of 149 respondents which is followed by 17.3 percent in student's category. 12.0 percent respondents are engaged in business, whereas 11.3 percent respondents are unemployed. 9.8 percent of the total population are engaged in government services, which is followed by 4.8 percent self-employed, 3.3 percent engaged in private jobs and 4.5 percent are in 'Others' category.

d. **Qualification:** The education level of the respondents shows that the highest 21.8 percent of the total respondents falls under 'illiterate' category. 20.5 percent of the respondents falls under 'post graduate and above' category, whereas 20.3 percent of the total respondents falls under 'matriculation' category who have passed 10th standard. 18.5 percent of the total population are graduate whereas 16.0 percent respondents falls 'under-matric' category and 3.0 percent respondents falls 'under-graduate' category, who are continuing with their study. Thus, based on the data, it is clear that majority of the illiterate and under matric respondents are belong to farmer's category, whereas many respondents whose qualification is 'post graduate and above' belong to unemployed category. Majority of the population who have passed class 10th standard and falls under matriculation category are engaged in business.

e. **Income of the respondents:** The annual income of the respondents has been classified into five sections i.e. less than 10,000, 10-50 thousand, 51-60 thousand, 61-99 thousand and 1 lakh and above. The data show that 33.3 percent of the total population falls under 'less than 10,000' category. This category mostly consist of students, unemployed and housewives. 32.8 percent of the respondents are earning 51-60 thousand, majority of them are farmers and few are business men/women. 24.5 percent of the respondents earns 61-99 thousand, most of them are farmers, business men/women and self-employed. 7.8 Percent respondent's falls under the category of 1 lakh and above, majority of them are government employees and business men/women and 1.8 percent of the total respondents are earning 10-50 thousand, they belong to farmer category.

f. **Marital status:** The marital status of the respondents has been classified into two sections i.e. married and unmarried. According to the survey, 63.7 percent of the total population falls under 'Married' category, whereas 36.3 percent respondents are 'Unmarried.' Most of the unmarried respondents are belong to unemployed and student category, while mostly married respondents are either farmer, government employees or business men/women. Based on the data, we can say that more married people are interested to listen to radio programmes in rural areas.

II. **Respondents access to mass media in rural areas**

Respondents access to mass media	Percentage	
	Yes	No
Respondent read newspapers	7.8 %	92.3 %
Respondent listen to radio	100 %	0 %
Respondent watching television	98.5 %	1.5 %
Respondent using cell phone	90.5 %	9.5 %

Enter Caption

The data indicate that 100 percent of the respondents listen to radio programmes even if they do not owned their personal radio set in houses they shares radio sets to listen to radio. 98.5 percent of the total population watch television in villages, whereas 90.5 percent respondents in rural areas are using cell phones for their daily communication. And only 7.8 percent of the total respondents are reading newspapers in villages.

Based on the above data, we can say that there are availability of newspapers, radio, television and cell phone in rural areas of Arunachal Pradesh, but majority of the rural populace prefer radio for information and educational purpose.

Also, According to **WSIS (2005)**, radio and television are all important forms of mainstream media. Because of their widespread application, the media are considered the most effective educational as well as socio-cultural tools. Depending on their educational needs, many nations can benefit from radio or even television in regard to informal learning.

III. **Respondents access information from mass media**

Table 2

Respondents access information from mass media	Percentage	
	Yes	No
Respondent access information from newspapers	7.8 %	92.3 %
Respondent access information from radio	99.3 %	0.8 %
Respondent access information from television	62.5 %	37.5 %
Respondent access information from Internet	36.5 %	63.5 %

Enter Caption

The data indicate that 99.3 percent of total population are accessing information from radio and majority of them are male and occupies farmer's category, who belongs to 25-34 and 45-54 age groups.

62.5 percent of total population are accessing information from television whereas 36.5 percent of the respondents accessing information from internet. And only 7.8 percent of the total respondents are accessing information from newspapers.

Based on the above data, we can say that majority of the rural masses are accessing information from radio, while newspapers become the least choice to access information in rural areas.

Similarly, **Nakabugu (2001)** says radio is a significant communication medium that has been proven to be among the most successful platform in stimulating agriculture as well as advancement in rural regions, while **Hussain (1997)** writes radio and television are by far the most impactful communication platforms for growth especially in rural areas.

According to **FAO (2001), r**adio is widely considered the most significant platform for connecting with developing-country rural communities. Among developing countries, radio has been widely employed as an academic platform. According to documented source information, it has financed educational projects in a wide range of academic disciplines and in a variety of nations.

IV. **Kinds of information and radio programmes listen on radio**

Table 3

Kinds of information and radio programmes listen on radio	Percentage	
	Yes	No
News bulletins, regional news, dialect News	78.5 %	21.5%
Talk shows on social issues	51.5 %	48.5 %
Local dialect programmes	48.8 %	51.2 %
Farmers programmes	40.5 %	59.5 %
Women related programmes	39.5 %	60.5 %
Good Morning Itanagar	28.7 %	71.3 %
Health related programmes	24.3 %	75.8 %
Good Evening Itanagar	14.2 %	85.8 %
Phone-in programmes	11.5 %	88.5 %
Children programmes	7.8 %	92.3 %

Enter Caption

The table shows that **78.5** percent of the total population do listen to news bulletins, regional news and dialect news on radio. It is clear that majority of the respondents in rural areas listen to news bulletins and regional news broadcast from radio in different indigenous dialects besides Hindi and English languages.

According to the data, 51.5 percent of total respondents listen to talk shows on social issues broadcast on radio, whereas 48.8 percent of the total population do listen to local dialect programmes broadcast on radio particularly from AIR Itanagar and AIR Pasighat.

40.5 percent of the total respondents listen to farmers programmes like *KrishiVigyan* broadcast on radio, whereas 39.5 percent of the total population listen to women related programmes on radio. 28.7 percent respondents of the total population listen to Good Morning Itanagar broadcast from AIR Itanagar and 24.3 percent respondents of the total population do listen to health programmes like 'SwasthPeCharcha' on radio. Only 11.5 percent of the total respondents listen to phone in programme and 7.8 percent of the total population listen to children programme broadcast on radio.

V. **Radio creating awareness and educating rural masses**

Topics	Percentage		
	Agree	Disagree	Cannot say
Radio progs create awareness on social and cultural issues	79.5 %	20.5 %	0 %
Radio progs educate people on safe drinking water, SBM and about hygiene and sanitation in rural areas	99.8 %	0.3 %	0 %
Radio progs spread awareness on importance of education	97.3 %	2.8 %	0 %
Radio progs on govt schemes help in enhancing economic status of rural masses	66.0 %	3.8 %	30.3 %

Enter Caption

The data indicate that 79.5 percent of the total population have agreed that radio programmes create awareness on social and cultural issues in rural areas.

According to the data, it is clear that 99.8 percent of the total population are agreed with the statement that 'radio programmes such as safe drinking water, SBM educate and brought awareness about hygiene and sanitation in villages.' Thus, based on the above data, we can say that radio programmes and spots on various issues of society like safe drinking water, SBM etc. influence the villagers to make their place neat and clean.

The data show that 97.3 percent of the total respondents have agreed that different radio progs based on education contributes and spread awareness on the importance of education for overall development in rural areas, whereas 66.0 percent respondents have agreed that radio programmes on govt schemes has helped in enhancing economic status of people in rural areas.

VI. **Radio's role to bring change in rural society**

Table 5

Topics	Percentage		
	Agree	Disagree	Cannot say
Radio has brought changes to raise women status in society	68.8 %	31.3 %	0 %
Women related radio progs like *MahilaJagat* educate village women of their empowerment	95.5 %	0 %	4.5 %
Radio educate rural masses regarding perfect age of marriage for girl child	62.5 %	37.5 %	0 %
Radio educate people in improving agri-horti production	84.8 %	0 %	15.3 %

Enter Caption

According to the data, 68.8 percent of the total respondents have agreed that radio has brought changes to raise women status in society. Moreover, 95.5 percent of the total population have agreed that the women related radio programmes like *MahilaJagat*educate village women of their empowerment. While, only 4.5 percent respondents are unable to decide and falls under 'cannot say' category.

According to the survey, 62.5 percent of the total population agreed that radio programmes educate rural masses to decide the perfect age of marriage especially for the girl child. Many of the respondents with this view are male in 45-54 age group and belong to farmer's category and illiterate in qualification. Based on the above data, it is clear that the people in rural areas are changing their mind-set towards girl child. The system of child marriage is almost nil in villages now a days. They want to empower their girl child in society by providing them good education.

The data show that 84.8 percent of the total respondents are agreed with the statement that radio programme based on agri-horticultural production help the villagers to improve their agricultural production. Thus, based on the above data, we can say that radio programmes on agri-horti production help the rural people to improve their economic status and financially empower them in society.

VII. **Radio help to educate rural masses**

Table 6

Topics	Percentage		
	Agree	Disagree	Cannot say
Radio help in preserving and documenting folk culture and literature	98.8 %	0 %	1.3 %
Youth based radio progs help to educate people in eradication of social menace	24.8 %	37.0 %	38.3 %
Radio is most influential tool for change and educate rural masses in society	82.3 %	6.3 %	11.5 %
Issues of the community addressed appropriately on radio	76.3 %	10.8 %	13.0 %

Enter Caption

The table indicates that 98.8 percent of the total population are agreed with the statement that 'Radio help in preserving and documenting folk culture and literature in society.'

24.8 percent of the total population are agreed that 'youth based radio programmes like *yuwavani* help in eradicating of social menace from society.

The table shows that 82.3 percent of the respondents are agreed that 'Radio is the most influential tool for different kinds of changes in society.' Many of the respondents who agreed with the statement are male who belong to farmer and student's category. Most of them are 25-34 and 45-54 age groups, whose qualification are either matriculation or post graduate and above category.

The table shows that 76.3 percent of the total population are agreed that the issues of the community such as health, hygiene, road, water, sanitation etc. are addressed appropriately on radio. Majority of the respondents who agreed with the statement are male who belong to farmer and student's category and many of them are either illiterate or post graduate and above in qualification.

VIII. **Conclusion**

IX. From the above discussion, it is clear that radio continues to play an important role in the growth of rural society in Arunachal Pradesh. It is the main medium of information to rural populace and makes them aware about various issues of society, government policies and schemesbecause of its wider reach in remote areas. There might be some language barrier with other mass media especially to rural people but in radio that broadcast programmesin the language of the listeners makes them easy to understand the information. They do not need to be literate to listen to radio programmes. Besides broadcasting news bulletins in local dialects, radio also broadcasts tribal folk music, talks, interviews and discussion on different social issues to make the rural people aware about their rights and other issues of society.

Despite the availability of television, radio, internet connectivity and newspapers (in few villages) in rural areas of Arunachal Pradesh, the people are active users of radio for accessing information, educational and also entertainment purpose. Though they owned television in their house and also access to internet connectivity but it depends on the regular electricity connection in the area. In remote villages where the access to other mass media is not possible, the rural people mostly rely on radio programmes for any kind of information and educating themselves.

The issues of society like public health and hygiene, sanitation, gender inequality, safe drinking water, immunization or vaccination programmes, right to education, save the girl child, social campaign like *betibachaobetipadao, paregadesh to baregadesh, harghardastak,* etc. broadcast from this traditional media channel help the rural people to get information about its update and happening.

X. **Suggestions** Being a multi-ethnic tribal state in the northeast India, Arunachal Pradesh has five radio stations located at Itanagar, Pasighat, Tawang, Tezu and Zirowhich are not sufficient to disseminate information about various social, political, economic and other events to the rural masses. Thus, adequate number of radio stations should be established at different suitable locations of the state. As there are 26 major tribes and more than 110 sub-tribes in the state, only 16 dialect programmes being broadcast from AIR Itanagar and Pasighatis very less and need to be expanded by including more Arunachalidialects that would disseminate information and also educate the rural masses about various issues of society, government schemes and policies in their own mother tongue.

XI.   **References**

XII.   http://www.arunachalipr.gov.in

XIII.   Wabwire, J. (2013). *The role of community radio in development of the rural poor. New Media and Mass Communication, 10, 2224-3267.*

XIV.   World Summit on the Information Society (WSIS) (2005). *Second Phase of the WSIS,16-18 November, 2005, Tunis.*

XV.   Nakabugu, S, B. (2001). *The Role of Rural Radio in Agricultural and Rural Development Translating Agricultural Research Information into Messages for Farm Audiences. Programme of the Workshop in Uganda, 19 February 2001.*

XVI.   Hussain, M.(1997). *Mass Media. In: Memon, R.A. and Basir, E. (eds.), Extension Methods, pp: 208–61. Islamabad, Pakistan:National Book Foundation.*

XVII.   FAO. (2001). *Knowledge and information for food security in Africa from traditional media to the Internet. Communication for Development Group, Sustainable Development Department. Rome: FAO.*